KU-355-616

PENGUIN PLAYS

PL 50

EPITAPH FOR GEORGE DILLON
THE KITCHEN
THE HAMLET OF STEPNEY GREEN

EPITAPH
FOR GEORGE DILLON

John Osborne and Anthony Creighton

*

THE KITCHEN

Arnold Wesker

*

THE HAMLET
OF STEPNEY GREEN

Bernard Kops

PENGUIN BOOKS

Penguin Books Ltd, Harmondsworth, Middlesex, England
Penguin Books Inc, 3300 Clipper Mill Road, Baltimore 11, Md, U.S.A.
Penguin Books Pty Ltd, Ringwood, Victoria, Australia

—

Epitaph for George Dillon
First published by Faber and Faber 1958
Published by Penguin Books 1960
Reprinted in this collection 1964
Copyright © John Osborne and Anthony Creighton, 1958

—

The Kitchen
First published by Penguin Books 1960
Reprinted in this collection 1964
Copyright © Arnold Wesker, 1960

—

The Hamlet of Stepney Green
First published by Penguin Books 1959
Reprinted 1960
Reprinted in this collection 1964
Copyright © Bernard Kops, 1959

—

Made and printed in Great Britain
by Western Printing Services Ltd
Bristol
Set in Monotype Bembo

Contents

JOHN OSBORNE AND
ANTHONY CREIGHTON

Epitaph for George Dillon

TO E.M.C.

WITH OUR LOVE

All professional inquiries in regard to this play should
be addressed to the authors' agent, Margery Vosper
Ltd, 32 Shaftesbury Avenue, London, w1, and all
amateur inquiries should be addressed to Messrs
Evans Brothers Ltd, Montague House, Russell
Square, London, wc1.

EPITAPH FOR GEORGE DILLON

First professionally presented at The Royal Court Theatre, London, on 11 February 1958, with the following cast:

JOSIE ELLIOT	Wendy Craig
RUTH GRAY	Yvonne Mitchell
MRS ELLIOT	Alison Leggat
NORAH ELLIOT	Avril Elgar
PERCY ELLIOT	Toke Townley
GEORGE DILLON	Robert Stephens
GEOFFREY COLWYN-STUART	Philip Locke
MR WEBB	Paul Bailey
BARNEY EVANS	Nigel Davenport

Directed by William Gaskill

The action of the play takes place in the home of the Elliot family just outside London.

ACT ONE

The home of the Elliot family, just outside London. Spring, late afternoon.
The action takes place in the sitting room and hall. The front door being
stage right. In the hall, immediately facing, are the stairs which turn off
left. Flat against the staircase is a hat and coat stand, shelving hats, coats,
magazines, umbrellas, etc., in the midst of which is a vase of everlasting
flowers. Upstage of the hall, under the arch formed by the stairs, is the door
leading into the room called the lounge. Next to this upstage is the invisible
wall which divides the hall from the sitting room. The only object suggesting
the wall is a door set upstage. Downstage of this, set against the 'wall' facing
into sitting room is a radiogram, upon which stands a biscuit barrel and a
silver-plated dish containing wax or real fruit. Nearby an arm-chair of the
'contemporary' kind faces downstage. Against the upstage wall, right, is a
dining chair. Centre, an ornate cocktail cabinet and another dining chair. On
the wall, flanking this, are two wall lights, in the centre of which is painted
a group of wild ducks in flight.

Left centre is the door leading to the kitchen, next to which is the kitchen
hatch, which, when raised, reveals the kitchen beyond. Below the hatch is a
tea-trolley. Above the hatch, on the wall, is a tinted photograph of a wedding
group. In the stage left wall, french windows which look out on to a small
back garden. Below the french windows, a half-round occasional table;
above hangs a mirror. In front of the french windows a settee, again of the
utility-contemporary period. At the head a white-painted wrought-iron
floor lamp. Upstage left centre, a draw-leaf table with dining chair and
arm-dining-chair in position. On the cocktail cabinet stands a large china
model of an alsatian dog, and a photograph of a soldier in a silver frame,
decorated with 'Haig' poppies.

[At rise of curtain, JOSIE is on stage alone. She is about twenty, pretty
in a hard, frilly way and nobody's fool. At the moment she is not
looking her best. The turban she is wearing reveals a couple of curlers
above her forehead, her jumper is grubby and her slacks baggy,

9

stained, and not very fetching. She is sprawled in the arm-chair. In a vicious idleness she stares at a highly coloured weekly. Mozart is on the radio, delicate, liquid. She flips through the magazine, is about to put it down when something catches her attention. She reads.]

JOSIE: Fancy writing up and asking *that*!

[*She laughs and goes on with her reading, fondling one of her curlers as she does so. Presently she throws the magazine down.*]

Soppy cow!

[*She sighs and leans back, thrusts her hands into the top of her slacks, rubbing her stomach and frowning. She gets up and stares at her reflection in the mirror. Pursing her lips experimentally, she watches the effect. She leans forward and tries fluffing up her eyebrows. It doesn't seem very successful and she sighs again.*]

Oh, that damn row!

[*She goes to the radio, stabs at the knobs, then gives up and switches it off. Her eye catches the magazine again and she goes through it again until she finds what she is looking for. She stares at it sullenly and flings the paper on the floor. At the mirror again she tries several grimaces, puts out her tongue. A little more speculation, and she goes over to the settee, and sinks down on her knees. She stretches, and, catching sight of the resulting white space between her jumper and slacks, strokes herself dreamily. She slides forward on to her stomach, her hands moving over the arm of the settee, curiosity in her fingers and boredom in her body. She starts to sing, in a studied, offhand way, one of those downward-inflection popular hits.*]

'Why don't you Give Me . . . Give Me . . .'

[*Pause.*]

'All that you have to share.

Why don't you Give Me . . . Give Me . . .'

[*She picks her nose daintily, and turns over on her back.*]

'And tell me you really c-are . . .'

[*Her hand trails the space beside her, like a hand in rippling water, then stops, as she says deliberately:*]

I wonder – what it *would* be like?

[*She is about to swing her legs above her head, when the front door bell rings.*]

Good-O!

[*She rushes off to the front door, almost reaches it when she remembers something, and comes back into the dining room. Her eyes light on her handbag, and she snatches it up, taking it with her, through the hall, straight to the front door. The bell is still ringing, and she calls out:*] Oh, all right! Wait a minute! Wait a minute! [*Opens front door.*] [*We hear a voice saying:* 'Parcel for Mrs Elliot. Three pounds fifteen and ninepence to pay.'] *Miss* Elliot, if you please. I thought you were never coming. Here you are. You have been a long time. I thought you'd have been here this morning. I haven't even been able to go up the road, waiting for you to come. What? I haven't got it. Well, you'll have to change it.

[*A few minutes of change-fumbling before she slams the front door and goes into the sitting room with a square cardboard box in her arms, which she starts to open excitedly, kneeling on the floor. Off comes the string and paper, then the lid and a layer of tissue paper. She rises quickly, places the box on the settee, takes a cigarette from her handbag, which she puts in her mouth, kicks off her slippers, and goes to the radiogram, unzipping her slacks at the same time. She raises the lid, switches it on, and takes off her slacks, leaving them on the floor, one leg inside out. She selects a record from the pile beside her, and puts it on. Cigarette in mouth, she waits expectantly until the corn-crake growl of a New Orleans trumpet strides off into a piece of fairly traditional jazz. She runs back to her parcel and takes out the contents, in a scurry of paper and impatience, which turn out to be a pair of black, tapering trousers. She puts them on, zipping up the sides with a little difficulty. Hands on hips, she looks down at the results anxiously then delightedly. She goes nearer to the mirror, to get a better view of herself. She bounces up and down, looking at this angle and that, patting her stomach, feeling the seat until she is finally satisfied. She lights her cigarette, then, putting her hands in her unfamiliar pockets,*] *strikes a more or less elegant attitude and a bored expression, one black undeniably slim leg straight out in front of the other. She inclines her head back, and blows out a cloud of smoke.* JOSIE *may be funny at times, but she is never consciously so. She begins to dance, slowly at first, and surprisingly well, across right, ending up by lying with her back on the floor, and her knees up. The front door opens, and* RUTH *enters hall.* JOSIE *sits up quickly.*]

That you, Mum?

[RUTH *closes the door, but makes no reply.* JOSIE *takes off her new trousers, and starts slipping them back in their box. As she is doing this,* RUTH *enters from the hall. She is about forty, slim, smartly dressed, attractive. She carries a small week-end case, which she puts down when she gets into the sitting room.*]

You're in early.

[RUTH *goes to the radiogram and switches it off.*]

RUTH: Do you mind if we do without New Orleans just for the moment?

[*She crosses and picks up Josie's old slacks from the floor.*]

Are you looking for these?

[*She throws them over, and* JOSIE *manages to catch them.*]

JOSIE: Thought you were Mum.

RUTH: I don't suppose you'd made any tea?

JOSIE [*putting on her slacks*]: I had some at dinner time.

[RUTH *goes into the kitchen, and puts the kettle on to boil.*]

You're in early.

RUTH [*off*]: Why aren't you at work today?

JOSIE: Wasn't feeling very good this morning.

RUTH [*off*]: Oh?

JOSIE: So Mum said I'd better stay indoors.

[*She is staring at the case Ruth has left on the floor.*]

Going on your holidays?

RUTH [*off*]: No – coming back. Satisfied?

JOSIE: How can you be coming back, when you haven't been away? Anyway, I haven't had a day off work for ages – it won't hurt them. [*Picking up the case to see if it is empty.*] New case?

RUTH [*off*]: I picked it up from where I left it last night – at Leicester Square Left Luggage Office. And it's full of obscene photographs.

JOSIE: Oh?

RUTH [*appearing in the doorway*]: Josie: give me a cigarette, will you? I came all the way back in the train without one. [*Back into kitchen.*] There wasn't any post for me was there?

JOSIE [*crossing to her handbag right*]: Package came for you – registered.

RUTH [*off*] No letters?

JOSIE: Just the pools. It's only a small one. Doesn't weigh anything hardly.

RUTH [*off*]: And what's inside it?

JOSIE [*searching in her handbag*]: How should I know?

RUTH [*off*]: Didn't you open it?

JOSIE: What do you mean? Course I didn't open it.

RUTH [*coming back in*]: If you must fry yourself food when you're feeling ill, you might have the decency to clear up afterwards. The gas stove is covered in grease and muck – it's filthy.

[*She takes off her hat, and moves to the occasional table down left, where she sees a small package.*]

Is this it? [*Examines it, and goes on, rather absently.*] You've even left the breakfast things in the sink.

[*JOSIE is holding her packet of cigarettes, watching her curiously. RUTH stares at the packet.*]

JOSIE: Typewritten.

RUTH: You've had damn-all to do all day. It's like a slum when your mother comes in.

JOSIE: Aren't you going to open it?

RUTH [*a quick glance at her*]: I said you're a slut.

JOSIE: Oh, did you? I didn't hear.

[*After a momentary hesitation, RUTH unwraps the package. JOSIE slips her cigarettes back into her handbag, and moves over to the*] *kitchen door. From a small cardboard box,* RUTH *takes out a man's wrist-watch.* JOSIE *takes it in, and goes into the kitchen.*]

JOSIE: I'll get a cup of tea.

[*The watch is lying in Ruth's hand, as with the other she takes out a piece of notepaper and reads it. Then she places the box on the table. She stares at the paper, stroking her temples with her fingers, as if she felt a weight in her head. Presently, she calls out to* JOSIE *in the kitchen. The edge has gone out of her voice, and she sounds tired.*]

RUTH: Josie: be a good girl and get me that cigarette, will you?

[JOSIE *enters with a cup of tea, which she hands to her.*]

JOSIE: That man was here again this afternoon, asking for you.

RUTH: I've asked you twice to let me have one of your cigarettes. Please! I'll pay you back tonight.

JOSIE: Haven't got one. Sorry.

RUTH [*turning back to the table*]: Oh well. I suppose I'll have to go upstairs, anyway. There may be some in the bedroom somewhere.

[*She replaces the watch and note in the little box.*]

Who was here, did you say?

JOSIE: That man. I don't know who he is. The one who came on Saturday, and again the other day. That's the third time he's been.

RUTH: I thought you told him I didn't get in till 5.30?

JOSIE: I did. He said he'd come back one evening.

RUTH [*to arm-chair and sitting*]: Well, what time did he come today?

JOSIE: About four, I suppose.

RUTH: He doesn't sound very bright, whoever he is. What's he look like?

JOSIE: Not bad. Bit like Frankie Vaughan.

RUTH: Who the hell's Frankie Vaughan? [*Sipping tea.*] You make a putrid cup of tea, don't you. Doesn't he say what he wants?

JOSIE: Just that he wants to see you – that's all.

RUTH: Strange way to go about it. Calling at the time when you've specifically told him I shall be out. You didn't tell him anything did you?

JOSIE: Tell him what? That he looked like Frankie Vaughan?

RUTH: Oh, Josie, for heaven's sake, can't you see I'm tired? All I want is a cigarette and a bath.

[*The front door opens and* MRS ELLIOT *comes in. She is a sincere, emotionally restrained little woman in her early fifties, who firmly believes that every cloud has a silver lining. She carries various carrier-bags filled with shopping. At the hall-stand she removes her coat.*]

RUTH: That's your mother. For heaven's sake make a start on that kitchen so that she can get started on the supper without having to clear up your mess first.

JOSIE [*moving to kitchen*]: O.K.

MRS ELLIOT: Are you there, Josie? [*Taking off hat.*]

JOSIE: Hullo, Mum. You're not in any trouble are you, Auntie?

RUTH: In trouble? Do you mean in the general or the popular sense?

JOSIE: What?

MRS ELLIOT [*coming into sitting room with bags*]: Hullo, dear, hullo Josie. Managed to get a seat on the train today, thank goodness. [*Into kitchen.*]

RUTH: Hullo, Kate.

JOSIE: Hullo, Mum.

MRS ELLIOT: Oh Josie, you are a naughty girl, you really are. [*Into sitting room.*] I was hoping you'd have everything nice and clean and tidy when I came in.

JOSIE: I was just going to do it.

MRS ELLIOT: Just look at it out there. It would be tonight too, when there's so much to do.

RUTH: Here, let me take that from you. [*Taking one of the bags.*]

MRS ELLIOT: Thank you, Ruth.

JOSIE: I'm sorry, Mum. Auntie Ruth was talking to me just as I was going to do it. Everyone seems a bit early tonight. [*Into kitchen.*]

MRS ELLIOT [*unpacking carrier*]: I asked Mr Beamish to let me off five minutes early. Didn't like it either. I thought I'd just miss the rush. Funny what a difference a few minutes makes. Anyway, I managed to get some shopping up the road before they closed.

Oh dear, what a rush. There we are. You're back early, Ruth dear. Weren't you feeling well? Wonder if George likes parsley sauce.

RUTH: It wasn't anything. Central heating in the office, I expect.

MRS ELLIOT: Well – Josie complained she wasn't too great this morning at breakfast time, so I made her stay at home. I hope you haven't gone and caught something off of her – food poisoning or something.

RUTH: Yes.

MRS ELLIOT: You do look tired, I must say.

RUTH: Oh, I'm better now. Josie gave her *Auntie* a cup of tea.

MRS ELLIOT: You always hate her calling you Auntie don't you. What can you expect dear when that's what you are? Now, I wanted you to do something for me. What was it? Josie, don't bother with those things now. Lay the table for me in here instead, there's a good girl.

RUTH: You seem a bit overloaded.

MRS ELLIOT: Well, I had to get a few extras.

JOSIE [*in from kitchen*]: Where's the fire, Mum?

MRS ELLIOT: Now try and help me a little, Josie. I'm rather cross with you over that kitchen, my girl.

JOSIE: Well, I'm doing it, aren't I?

RUTH: All right you two, I'll help, only don't go on about it, please. [*Into kitchen.*]

JOSIE: Well, she was 'going on' a bit herself just now.

MRS ELLIOT: That's enough, Josie. [*Clearing table.*] I had hoped that at least you could have had the table laid.

JOSIE: Yes, Mum, all right.

MRS ELLIOT: I'm in such a muddle, I don't know where I am. I haven't a chance to do a thing. Hope your father comes in on time.

JOSIE: What's all the panic? Don't tell me you've got somebody coming?

MRS ELLIOT: Yes, I have.

JOSIE: Who on earth is it?

[RUTH *comes in with loaded tray and puts it down, and she and* MRS ELLIOT *start laying the table.*]

MRS ELLIOT: Young George is coming, that's all.

RUTH: George?

MRS ELLIOT: George Dillon. The young fellow that works at my place. You know. I told you about him.

RUTH: Oh, did you? I don't remember.

JOSIE: Oh, him. [*She yawns loudly and flops into the arm-chair.*]

MRS ELLIOT: Of course I told you. I've often spoken about him. I've asked him down to tea lots of times. But each time some appointment seems to turn up and he can't come. Well, he's coming now, for certain. He's a very busy chap. Always on the go.

RUTH: Oh, that one. The rather superior young man who's so much younger than the rest of you. Is he still there? I thought you said the job wasn't quite good enough for him?

MRS ELLIOT: I've always felt a bit sorry for him, that's all. He seemed so much on his own all the time. And, one day, I started telling him about our Raymond, and he was most interested. He was in the services as well, you see.

RUTH: Quite a coincidence.

MRS ELLIOT: Yes. He went right through the war.

RUTH: I had the idea we all did.

[*Pause.*]

MRS ELLIOT: No, Ruth, some boys didn't get to see the end of it.

RUTH: I'm sorry, Kate. I've had a bit of a day, I'm afraid. I'm not in the right frame of mind to talk to young men, refined or not. If I can't do anything for you down here, I'll go and run myself a bath, if you don't mind.

MRS ELLIOT: Oh! Were you going to have a bath now?

RUTH: Yes. Why?

MRS ELLIOT: Well, I can't go into a long rigmarole now – I've too much to do before George comes. But you see – well, you've got to know sometime, I suppose – I've asked him to stay.

JOSIE: Stay? What, here?

MRS ELLIOT: It won't be for long – just till he finds somewhere else to go.

JOSIE: What's wrong with where he is?

MRS ELLIOT: He's not very happy there. I'll tell you later. Don't worry me with a lot of questions now, Josie. There's too much to do.

RUTH: Well, it's your business. It's your house – not mine. What about Percy?

MRS ELLIOT: Nothing about Percy. It's got nothing to do with him.

RUTH: Your're right, of course. [Rather dryly.] It isn't his house, either.

MRS ELLIOT: There's just one thing –

JOSIE: There won't half be an atmosphere when he finds out. You know what Dad's like – he hasn't got over those budgerigars you bought yet.

MRS ELLIOT: He knows what he can do, and it won't take me long to tell him. Oh, do clear up that paper and stuff, Josie. The place looks awful. What was I saying?

RUTH: 'There's just one thing.'

MRS ELLIOT: Oh yes, Ruth. I was going to ask if you would mind very much moving out of your room for a few days, and going in with Norah.

RUTH: Why yes, I do mind. Is it really necessary? Does George Whats-his-name have to have my room?

MRS ELLIOT: No, he doesn't have to, but I thought it would be nicer – being Ray's old room, he'd like it. More like a man's room. Still –

RUTH [quietly]: You know, I do like to have at least some time to myself. And anyway, Norah sleeps with her mouth open.

MRS ELLIOT: Oh, very well, Ruth. Josie can go in with her. You won't mind, will you, Josie?

JOSIE [folding up paper]: Oh, all right. All this blessed fuss! [Into kitchen.]

RUTH: I'm sorry, Kate, but you do understand.

MRS ELLIOT: Never mind. I just thought it would be nicer, that's all.

It doesn't matter, dear. And there's no fuss, Madame Josie, thank you. God pays debts without money, I always say.

RUTH: You haven't any aspirin, have you? I don't seem to know where any of my things are –

MRS ELLIOT: There are some in the medicine chest, I think. And if you're going up, would you mind getting some of Josie's stuff into Norah's room – as that's going to be the arrangement?

RUTH: Right.

[*She is lost in her own thoughts and does not move.* MRS ELLIOT *is too preoccupied to notice. Pause.*]

MRS ELLIOT: Only would you mind doing it now, while Josie and I get straight down here? George'll be here very soon – he's only got to pick up his bags from his digs. Is that your case?

RUTH [*picking it up, and into hall*]: I'll take it up with me. [*Taking off scarf and hanging it up.*] Is there anything else?

MRS ELLIOT: No, thank you very much, Ruth. I must get started now.

[RUTH *goes upstairs.*]

Oh, yes – [*into hall*] – Ruth, dear, would you put a clean towel in the bathroom for George? I expect he'd like a wash when he comes in.

RUTH [*halfway upstairs*]: Yes.

MRS ELLIOT: I'm sorry you're not feeling well, dear.

[RUTH *goes on upstairs.* MRS ELLIOT *returns to sitting room.*]

MRS ELLIOT: Now where are we?

[*The table by now is almost laid, and* MRS ELLIOT *completes it.*]

JOSIE [*in from kitchen*]: Will it be the boiled pork, Mum? There isn't much left – least, not after Dad gets his hands on it.

MRS ELLIOT: He can have it all, as far as I'm concerned. Anyway, it won't worry George, he's a vegetarian. [*To cocktail cabinet.*]

JOSIE: A what?

MRS ELLIOT [*triumphantly*]: A vegetarian. Now, where's the sherry got to, I wonder? Oh, yes.

[*She finds the bottle, and puts it on the table.*]

JOSIE: Oh, one of them. He sounds a bit wishy-washy to me.

MRS ELLIOT: Well, he's not – he's a real gentleman.

JOSIE: That's what I mean. My, we are going posh, aren't we? Sherry! Anybody'd think it was Christmas.

MRS ELLIOT [to kitchen]: That's enough of that, young lady. Now go and get dressed and make yourself a bit more presentable, or else George will think I brought you up in the slums.

JOSIE [idly round the room]: George, George, George. Georgie Porgie puddeny-pie, kissed the girls and made then cry –

MRS ELLIOT [from kitchen]: Now do as I say, dear, please.

JOSIE: All right, Mum. [She starts to sing.]

> 'Why don't you Give me . . .
> Give Me. Give Me . . .
> All that you –
> All that you
> Have to share . . .'

[Her eyes light on the small package on the table down left. She moves over to it. She extracts the note from the package, and unfolds it.]

MRS ELLIOT [off]: Draw the curtains before you go, will you, dear? Thank goodness the days are drawing out again, though. I'm so sick of the winter.

JOSIE: O.K., Mum.

[She moves to the french windows left, draws one of the curtains, and begins reading the letter.]

[Reading] 'My dear – You have just left, and I have found that you have *left* two pounds for me on the desk. How thoughtful of you, and, after that catechism of smug deficiencies you had just recited to me, how very practical and how like you. I suppose you must have slipped it there while I was swallowed up in the damned misery of our situation. Make no mistake – for the money, I'm grateful. But your setting up as a kind of emotional soup kitchen makes me spit.

[JOSIE is seen to fold her arms to her and shiver.]

If you had any understanding at all, you would know what a bitter taste this kind of watery gruel must have. This is the Brown Windsor of love all right, and the only fit place for it is the sink. If this is the kind of thing you and your pals dole out for the proletariat and its poor, grubby artists, you had better think again. I'm just going out for some beer. PS. Was just going to post this, when I thought I would return this watch to you. It seems to be the one thing I have left that you ever gave me. I'd like to think that my returning it would hurt you, but I know it won't.'

[*Bell rings. The lights in the sitting room blaze on.* MRS ELLIOT *has switched them on. The door bell goes on ringing furiously.*]

MRS ELLIOT: My goodness, Josie, can't you please answer the front door for me? I've got milk on the stove. [*Into kitchen.*] And I asked you to draw those curtains, didn't I?

JOSIE: O.K. [*Draws curtains.*] All right, all right, I'm coming.
[*Goes through hall to front door.*]
Oh, it's you. It's only Norah, Mum.

[NORAH *comes in, wearing outdoor clothes. She is in her middle thirties. She has some of her mother's restraint but this is due more to having 'been let down twice'. There is no bitterness, only a naïve simplicity in all things and at all times.*]

MRS ELLIOT: That you, Norah?

JOSIE [*going into sitting room*]: Well, I've just said so, haven't I?

NORAH [*following her*]: Can't think where I left my key. It's probably in my other bag. I'll have a look in a minute. [*Takes off hat and coat.*] Blessed train, packed as usual. [*Fetches her slippers from under the settee and changes her shoes.*] I saw Father coming up the road, but I wasn't going to wait for *him* to let me in. Not after this morning.

[JOSIE *takes out her 'jazz' trousers and holds them against her waist dancing and humming quietly.*]

MRS ELLIOT [*in kitchen*]: Had a nice day, dear?

NORAH: Not bad, thanks, Mum. [*To Josie*] You going to the club tonight?

JOSIE: I might. Why?

NORAH: Nothing.

JOSIE: Len's got a new motor-bike. It's a smasher.

NORAH: Fancy.

JOSIE: Mum says he can come to dinner on Sunday.

MRS ELLIOT [*in from kitchen*]: Well, Mum has changed her mind. He can't.

JOSIE: Oh, Mum! Why?

MRS ELLIOT: I'll tell you why later. For goodness' sake take that blessed box upstairs. Supper's nearly ready and there's only George and him to come.

[JOSIE *picks up box and trousers and goes upstairs, singing her favourite song.*]

NORAH: George who?

MRS ELLIOT: Young George from the office, you know the one who gave me the necklace.

NORAH: Oh, him.

MRS ELLIOT: Would you like to start your supper, dear? It's all ready, and I expect you're hungry. [*She goes into the kitchen.*]

NORAH: You know I'm never hungry, Mum.

MRS ELLIOT: Too many sweets, my girl, that's your trouble.

[NORAH *sits at her usual place at the table.*]

MRS ELLIOT: You know what a state your teeth are in already. [*In with a plate of food which she places in front of Norah.*] I'm sure those sweets are half the trouble. There, see how you like that.

NORAH: Thanks, Mum.

[MRS ELLIOT *goes to the foot of stairs and calls.*]

MRS ELLIOT: Ruth – Ruth, dear! Don't be long will you? And don't forget that towel. [*She returns to sitting room.*] Is it all right, dear?

NORAH: Yes, thanks.

MRS ELLIOT: That's good.

[MRS ELLIOT *goes into kitchen as the front door opens.* PERCY, *her husband, comes in with a brief-case, mac, and umbrella, all of which he deposits at the hat-stand. He is a small, mean little man. Small in every sense of the word, with a small man's aggression. He goes upstairs.*]

NORAH: Mum!

MRS ELLIOT [*coming in*]: Yes, dear? Something wrong?

NORAH: *He's* just come in, I think.

MRS ELLIOT: Oh! [*Going to foot of stairs.*] Percy! – Was that you, Percy? [*She returns to sitting room.*] I suppose it was him, Norah?

NORAH: Of course it was. I'd know that cat-like tread anywhere. Trust him not to give a civil answer to a civil question.

MRS ELLIOT: The only time your father ever gave a civil answer to a civil question was when he said 'I will' at the wedding. Hope George isn't long, then we can all clear off into the lounge and watch the telly – leave your father to it. Anything on tonight? Not one of them morbid plays, I hope.

NORAH: There's some skating, I think.

MRS ELLIOT: That'll be nice. [*Into kitchen.*] They usually have some nice music with that.

[PERCY *comes downstairs and, after taking an evening paper from his brief-case, goes into the sitting room and sits at the table in the arm-dining-chair.*]

MRS ELLIOT [*lifting kitchen hatch*]: Will you have boiled pork or boiled eggs?

PERCY [*reading paper*]: Nothing.

MRS ELLIOT: You heard what I said – boiled pork or boiled eggs?

PERCY: And you heard what I said – nothing. Just a cup of tea.

[MRS ELLIOT *slams down hatch.* NORAH *pours out tea for her father and herself.*]

NORAH: Must put some more water in the pot.

PERCY: You'll drown it.

NORAH: And I know something else that needs drowning.

[*Into kitchen with teapot.* MRS ELLIOT *comes in with plate of food, and sets it in front of Percy.*]

PERCY: I said I didn't want anything.

MRS ELLIOT: You'll no doubt eat it just the same. Josie! Ruth! Come along, now! And another thing: I hope you'll mind your manners, Percy, in future, particularly as I have a young gentleman from the office coming to stay here for a little while. [*To herself.*] It'll be like having Raymond in the house again.

PERCY: Accch! So you've taken to cradle-snatching, have you? Not content with taking another woman's husband, you have to pick up a 'young gentleman' as well. Where did all this happen – Dean Street?

MRS ELLIOT [*with an effort*]: Look, Percy, I'm warning you, once and for all, this is *my* house, and I have worked for every penny I bought it with, and everything in it. As far as I'm concerned, you're just the lodger here. Why you've got your knife into Jack Livings, goodness only knows. They're nice, respectable people, and well you know it. I'm sure I don't know what Mrs Livings would say if she knew about your horrible accusations. Just because Mr Livings comes in now and again to do a few useful things about the house, that's all it is – things you're too *damn* lazy to do for me.

NORAH [*mildly*]: Mum!

MRS ELLIOT: I'm sorry, Norah, but there it is. There are times when your father goes too far with his insults. And I'll have you know this too: George is a fine, clean, upright young man. And he's clever too. He's in the theatrical line, he is, and one day he's going to be as famous as that Laurence Olivier, you see, and then perhaps you'll laugh on the other side of your face.

PERCY: Accch! Theatrical line! Don't give me that nonsense. I bet you he hasn't got two ha'pennies for a penny – they never have, these people.

MRS ELLIOT: No – it's true that, at the moment, he hasn't a lot of money to throw around, but he will have, he's that type. He's used to money, you can tell that. He's very cultured.

NORAH: Not like some people we know.

PERCY: How is it he's only a tuppenny-ha'penny penpusher then?

MRS ELLIOT: He's not a clerk any longer. There was a little upset at the office today and he walked out. And a good job too, I say. Wasting his time and talent in a place like that. It's not right, and

I wouldn't like to see any boy of mine going to waste like that – especially when George has so many plans and ideas to make himself famous. There isn't much he can't turn his hand to in the theatrical line, believe me. Why he doesn't only act in plays, he writes them as well. As a matter of fact, he's bang in the middle of one at the moment. I expect he'll finish it while he's here.

PERCY: That's all very interesting, I'm sure. You've got it all nicely worked out between you, haven't you? But what about me? I'm going to look a proper bloody fool, aren't I? What are the neighbours going to think, I'd like to know?

MRS ELLIOT: No more than they do now, believe me. They know very well what you're like. I haven't forgotten yesterday either – shouting and swearing at the top of your voice. At the front door too. The humiliation of it! I don't mind you swearing at the back door, but the front door – well –

PERCY: Accch! You women – nag, nag, nag.

[JOSIE *comes downstairs, and goes into the 'lounge'. She is now 'respectable'.*]

MRS ELLIOT: Is that you, Ruth? Josie? Oh, for heaven's sake don't start looking at that thing till we've had supper.

[JOSIE *comes out of lounge into sitting room.*]

JOSIE: Oh, all right. It's only the newsreel.

[*She gets a chair and sits at the table.* MRS ELLIOT *goes into the kitchen and returns immediately with two plates of food.*]

It's panel-game night, isn't it?

MRS ELLIOT: There you are. [*She places plate in front of Josie.*] And I may as well have mine while I'm about it. And what do you say, Miss Josie? [*Sits at table.*]

JOSIE: Sorry. Thanks, Mum.

MRS ELLIOT: That's better.

[*They are all eating now. Pause.*]

JOSIE: Silence in the pig-market, let the old sow speak first.

MRS ELLIOT: Pudding, Percy?

PERCY: No.

JOSIE: Trouble with you, Dad, is you talk too much.

PERCY: Accch!

JOSIE: Can I put a record on, liven things up a bit. Ever so sordid in here, like a mortuary.

PERCY: That blessed racket. If I had my way –

MRS ELLIOT: It's Norah's wireless.

[JOSIE *puts on a record and returns to her seat.*]

JOSIE: The girls are taking a coach up to Salisbury on Sunday. You coming, Mum?

[RUTH *comes slowly down the stairs. Halfway down, there is a knock at the door.*]

MRS ELLIOT: No, I don't think so, dear. I expect Norah will though. She's coach mad.

[RUTH *answers the front door and a man's voice is heard outside. It is* GEORGE DILLON.]

NORAH: That would be lovely.

GEORGE: I'm awfully sorry, but does Mrs Elliot live here?

RUTH: Yes, she does. Did you want to speak to her?

GEORGE: Well, as a matter of fact she asked me to –

RUTH: Oh, I am sorry. Of course, you must be George. Do come in.

[GEORGE DILLON *enters. He is a little over thirty, boyish, yet still every year his age. He is short, not good-looking, but with an anti-romantic kind of charm. He displays at different times a mercurial, ironic passion, lethargy, offensiveness, blatant sincerity, and a mentally picaresque dishonesty – sometimes almost all of these at the same time. A walking confliction in fact. Just at the moment he is rather shy, feeling his way. He is carrying a suitcase and a 'carry-all' bag.*]

GEORGE: Yes, that's right. Thank you.

RUTH: I'm Ruth Gray. Mrs Elliot's sister.

GEORGE: How do you do?

[*They shake hands.*]

I seem to think we've met somewhere before, haven't we?

RUTH: Yes, I had that feeling too.

MRS ELLIOT: There's someone in the hall. Is that you, Ruth? [*She rises and goes into the hall.*]

RUTH: Mr Dillon has arrived, Kate.

MRS ELLIOT: Oh, good. You found your way all right, then? Glad you remembered it was Targon Wood station you had to get out at – most people think Pelham Junction is nearer, but it isn't really. I didn't hear you ring the bell. I expect you're hungry, aren't you? Would you like a wash before supper? Bring your things up. [*Going upstairs.*] I'll show you where your room is and where you can find the toilet.

[GEORGE *follows her up.*]

GEORGE: That's very nice of you. I couldn't find the bell, so I knocked instead.

MRS ELLIOT: Yes, I thought I didn't hear you ring.

[*They both disappear.* RUTH *stands looking up the stairs for a moment.*]

JOSIE: Must be nearly time for 'Classics on Ice'. I'm going to get a good seat before that fellow pinches it. [*Rising, she puts chair under table.*] Sounds ever so posh, doesn't he?

NORAH: I thought you were going to the club.

JOSIE: It's a woman's privilege to change her mind. [*Crosses into hall.*] Well, what's he like, Auntie? [RUTH *does not move.*] Auntie, what's he like?

RUTH: I don't know. Of course I don't. Why should I?

JOSIE: Oh, all right. I was only asking. Keep your hair on. [*Goes into lounge.*]

[RUTH *walks slowly into sitting room and sits in arm-chair.* NORAH *collects dirty plates.* PERCY *is still reading.* MRS ELLIOT *comes downstairs into sitting room.*]

MRS ELLIOT: Well, that's that. Have you finished, Percy?

[PERCY *folds newspaper.*]

PERCY: Where's Henry Irving?

MRS ELLIOT: Never you mind. I'd be grateful if you made yourself useful for once and made up the lounge fire.

[PERCY *rises and switches off radiogram and goes into lounge.* NORAH *takes things into the kitchen.*]

That's right, dear. Can't keep his hands off that wireless, can he? Now, Ruth, what about your supper, dear?

RUTH [*rising*]: Oh, nothing for me, thanks. [*Crosses to small table.*] I think I'll just have some hot milk and go to bed. [*She picks up the small package containing the watch. The note is missing.*] Kate.

MRS ELLIOT: Yes dear? Why, Ruth, what is it? You look quite pale. If I were you –

RUTH: Has anyone been at this table at all? Have they, Kate?

MRS ELLIOT: My dear, I'm sure I don't know. What a funny thing to ask. Why shouldn't they if they want to?

RUTH: There was a letter of mine here. Quite personal. A private letter. Someone has moved it.

MRS ELLIOT: Now, Ruth, dear, don't go upsetting yourself over a little thing like that. I expect you'll come across it later on. You go upstairs and I'll bring you up some hot milk later on.

[MRS ELLIOT *goes into the kitchen. Then* RUTH *goes into hall, halfway upstairs she stops for a moment, then comes down again, goes to lounge door, opens it, and calls. There is the sound of the 'Skater's Waltz' from within.*]

RUTH: Josie, come here a minute, will you?

JOSIE: Oh, what do you want, can't you see I'm watching the telly?

RUTH: Come here, please, when I ask you. [*She moves to the foot of the stairs as she waits.*]

JOSIE [*at lounge door*]: What do you want?

RUTH: Shut the door and come here.

[JOSIE *goes to her.*]

JOSIE: Well?

RUTH: Where is it?

JOSIE: Where's what? I don't know what you're talking about.

RUTH: You know damn well what. Give me that letter.

JOSIE: Oh, that. Oh, yes. [*Slowly, reluctantly, she withdraws letter from her jumper.*]

RUTH: Thank you very much. Kindly learn to keep your nose clean in future, will you?

JOSIE: So that's where you've been all these week-ends, with Jock. Does he wear a kilt?

RUTH: Mind your own damned business. [*Gives her a resounding smack across the face.*]

[*JOSIE yells. Enter* MRS ELLIOT.]

MRS ELLIOT: Why, whatever's going on?

JOSIE: Going on! It's Auntie Ruth what's been going on. *Carrying* on more like – with a man – and paying him for it what's more.

RUTH: Just you dare read my letters again, and I'll do more than slap your face.

JOSIE: Don't you talk to me like that – you're not my Mum.

MRS ELLIOT: If what Ruth says is true, Josie, then I'm very ashamed. I thought I'd brought you up to behave like a lady. Never, never do that again, do you hear? Now kindly leave the room – but first say you're sorry to Auntie Ruth.

JOSIE [*after some hesitation*]: I'm sorry, Auntie Ruth. [*Goes off to lounge singing 'If Jock could love me, love me. . . .'*]

RUTH: Slut! slut! slut!

MRS ELLIOT: Ruth – that's no way to talk, and you know it. [RUTH *turns away.*]

MRS ELLIOT: So things didn't work out then?

RUTH: No – I've just walked out on him, for better or for worse.

MRS ELLIOT: But I don't understand. Josie said something about paying him –

RUTH: I don't have to buy my love – or do I? Yes, I gave him the odd pound or two, to keep him alive.

MRS ELLIOT: But surely he could do a job of work?

RUTH: Job of work? He's a writer – the original starving artist in the attic – and I believed he had promise.

MRS ELLIOT: Then why did you leave him?

RUTH: He's been a promising young man for too long. Youthful promise doesn't look too well with receding hair. I've misjudged him – he's the complete flop, and I've spent nearly six years giving all I could to him, giving my love to him – such as it is.

MRS ELLIOT: It's beyond me, dear. It's funny – you're the only one in the family who doesn't have patience or understanding. While you were enjoying yourself at college, we all had to go out to work. I can only say that college gave you a lot of funny ideas.

RUTH: That's right. Funny enough to make me do an inexcusable thing. When he told me he hadn't a penny, not even the price of a packet of cigarettes, I went to his jacket pocket, and inside I found a cheque for eight guineas for some book review or other he'd written. He hadn't even told me about it. Not only did he lie about the money, but he even kept his piffling little success from me. A brainless, cheap little lie. And that did it – the whole works collapsed, the whole flimsy works. [*She walks to the door.*] I suppose that's really why I left him. [*Exits upstairs.*]

MRS ELLIOT [*crossing to hallway*]: George! Supper's ready, dear. [*Returns to kitchen.*]

[GEORGE *comes down, looking over his shoulder. As* GEORGE *crosses hall,* NORAH *comes out of kitchen into hall. 'Skater's Waltz' comes up good and loud.*]

NORAH: Hullo.

GEORGE: Hullo.

NORAH: Your supper's in there. I'm going to watch the skating. [*She goes into lounge.*]

[GEORGE *goes into sitting room. He coughs slightly.*]

MRS ELLIOT: That's right, dear, make yourself at home. Oh, that blessed telly, it's much too loud, isn't it? [*She crosses to lounge and opens door.*] Do put that telly down a bit, there's good children. We can't hear ourselves think in here. [*She goes back into sitting room.*] There, that's better isn't it? You sit there, dear. [*He sits in Percy's place.*] They're all watching the telly, so you can have your supper in peace. And while we're alone, dear – I want you to treat this just as if it were your home, just do whatever you like, won't you?

GEORGE: That's very kind of you, Mrs Elliot. I just don't know what to say [*he puts out his hand*]. I can only say that I won't impose myself on you for one minute longer than I can help. You're so very kind.

MRS ELLIOT: I've never mentioned this before, but I'm helping you all I can because I feel that in some small way I'm helping my son, Raymond. He was killed in the war, you know. That's his picture over there.

GEORGE: Yes, I'm sorry.

MRS ELLIOT [*very simply*]: He was a lovely boy. Clever, like you, artistic, too, but somehow he didn't seem to have that drive, that sort of initiative. Well, he didn't really have much chance to get on. But *you* will, George, I'm sure. With all your talent, you just can't go wrong. You're always planning things – and all the things you've already done too. You've got your acting and your plays and I don't know what, haven't you?

GEORGE: Oh, yes, Mrs Elliot, don't you worry – the play I'm writing now is just about in the bag. I can finish it in no time here. And I've already got someone interested in it – for the West End, I mean.

MRS ELLIOT: Well, there you are – what did I say? You certainly are one for irons in the fire, aren't you? And to think we shall all come and see your piece, and sit in the posh seats. That will be nice. Well, there we are, dear. And if Ray was here now, I'd be talking to him just as I'm talking to you. What I'm trying to say is that I want you to feel that you are taking his place in the home, and if there's anything you want – anything – please don't hesitate to ask. And don't, please, ever go short of money. Ray used to send me home so much a week when he was in the army, for me to save for him when he came home. I'd like to think it's being put to good use at last by helping you.

GEORGE: Bless you, Mrs Elliot. [*He coughs slightly.*] You're so very kind and thoughtful. I just don't know how to thank you. I only hope I'll prove worthy of your kindness. I promise I won't let you down in any way. I promise you that.

MRS ELLIOT [*patting his cheek*]: Good. Now we must see about getting you something to eat. Being a vegetarian you must eat lots of strange things. You'll have to tell me about them as we go along. [*Into kitchen.*]

GEORGE: I don't want you to put yourself out.

[*He sits looking around him.*]

MRS ELLIOT [*lifting hatch*]: I've got some nice boiled cod and parsley sauce. You do eat fish, don't you? [*She sees him staring at the birds on the wall, centre.*] Yes, Ray painted those. I told you he was artistic, didn't I?

[*Hatch down.* GEORGE *rises and walks round the room restlessly looking at the photographs on the wall, the cocktail cabinet, the general dressings. He then picks up the photograph of Raymond and looks at it steadily.*]

GEORGE: You stupid-looking bastard.

QUICK CURTAIN

ACT TWO

Summer. There is now a telephone standing on small table in hall. The french windows are open. The settee brought round to face slightly downstage.

> [NORAH, JOSIE, MRS ELLIOT, *and* PERCY *are sitting in their customary places at the meal table, eating. After curtain rises, a slight pause.*]

MRS ELLIOT: Pudding, Percy?

PERCY: No.

> [MRS ELLIOT *rises, taking plates into kitchen. As she does so, the telephone rings and she stops dead.*]

NORAH [*with awe*]: It's ringing!

JOSIE: The phone's ringing!

MRS ELLIOT: Our first call.

PERCY: What a racket – wireless, T.V., and now the blinking telephone.

MRS ELLIOT: Who's it for, I wonder?

NORAH: Answer it and see.

JOSIE: Yes, that's the best way to find out. [*Jumps up and goes into hall.*] I'll go, Mum. [*Lifts receiver.*] Yes, yes it is. Who? Yes. All right, I'll fetch her. [*Into sitting room*] It's for you, Mum. Ever such a funny man – he's got a sort of Chinese accent.

MRS ELLIOT [*giving plates to* JOSIE]: Chinese?

JOSIE: Yes.

MRS ELLIOT: But I don't know any Chinamen.

JOSIE: Well, you'd better hurry up and answer it, Mum – he's waiting.

NORAH: Perhaps he's from *Chu Chin Chow on Ice.*

> [MRS ELLIOT *goes into hall, and picks up receiver.*]

MRS ELLIOT: Hullo. Yes, it is. [JOSIE *stands in doorway listening.*]

Have we what? Well, I don't know. I'll see. [*To Josie*] He wants to know if we've got any laundry that wants doing. [*In phone*] No, I don't think so, thank you. What are you laughing at? [*She laughs.*] Oh, you are a naughty boy, you really are – you took us all in. [*To Josie.*] It's George.

JOSIE: Oh, silly. [*She goes into kitchen.*]

MRS ELLIOT: What's that, dear? Have you? Oh, I am pleased. Yes, oh we will! All right, dear. Good-bye. [*Replaces receiver, goes into sitting room.*] Says he's got some good news – he's got a job, and something about his play. I didn't quite catch what it was. Fancy young George being the first to ring up – and I had it put in specially for him too. Isn't that nice? Oh, I must sit down a minute – the excitement's too much for me!

[NORAH *pours tea.*]

NORAH: Needs more water. [*Into kitchen.*]

PERCY: *What's* he gone and got?

MRS ELLIOT: You heard, didn't you? A job. What did you think it was?

JOSIE [*in from kitchen*]: Must be something good for him to ring up like that.

MRS ELLIOT: Yes – silly boy. He was only at the station. He'll be home in a minute. I'm so glad. That awful day he left that office, he swore he'd stick it out until he got something really worth while.

[NORAH *comes in with teapot.*]

MRS ELLIOT: And it's turned up at last. He always said he wouldn't take anything tatty.

NORAH: What's 'tatty'?

MRS ELLIOT: I don't really know, dear – George is always saying it.

JOSIE: Well, now I can really tell the whole of Targon Broadway that we've got a real actor staying with us. That's if he doesn't get too stuck up, and want to go and live in Berkeley Square or something.

MRS ELLIOT: Of course he won't. George has settled down here

34

very well. This is his home now. There's no reason at all why he should have to go.

JOSIE: Well, he'll have to get married sometime, won't he?

MRS ELLIOT: Well, yes, there is that, of course.

NORAH: How do you know he hasn't got a girl friend already? [*Phone rings.*]

MRS ELLIOT: Well! There it is again – twice in a couple of minutes. [JOSIE *goes to it quickly, lifts receiver.*]

JOSIE [*on phone*]: Hullo. Who? No, I think you must have the wrong number. You're welcome. [*Puts phone down and returns to sitting room.*] Wrong number.

MRS ELLIOT: Oh.

JOSIE: What were we talking about?

MRS ELLIOT: George. I was just going to say that I think you're a bit gone on him aren't you. What about poor old Len Cook now, eh!

JOSIE: Well, George will do to fill in while Len does his National Service. I wouldn't mind going to Germany with Len though.

NORAH: You'd have to marry him first, wouldn't you? I mean it wouldn't be very proper just to go and – well – 'live' with him –

JOSIE: Oh, I don't know. I don't mind what I do or where I go, so long as my man's got money.

PERCY: The trouble with young girls today is that they spend too much time thinking about love and S-E-X.

JOSIE: S-E-X? Oh, sex. Sex doesn't mean a thing to me. To my way of thinking, love is the most important and beautiful thing in this world and that's got nothing to do with sex.

PERCY [*producing irrelevances like a bombshell*]: Well, I may be a crank and all that, but if I can persuade the counsel to close the park gates after dark, I shall die a happy man.

NORAH: What on earth's that got to do with sex?

MRS ELLIOT: Well, I don't think we need go on with this conversation – but Josie is quite right. You keep those beautiful thoughts dear and you can be sure you won't come to any harm. Put the kettle on for George, there's a dear. [JOSIE *goes into kitchen.*]

[GEORGE *appears at the french window, waving a bottle of wine.*]

GEORGE: Friends, Romans, and countrymen, lend me your ears!

MRS ELLIOT: Oh, George! You did make me jump! [GEORGE *goes up and hugs her.*] And I'm so pleased about your job dear – we're all dying to hear about it.

JOSIE: Where is it, George, Drury Lane?

GEORGE: Could be, Josie, could be! Come on Norah, cheer up and find the corkscrew for the big Bacchanalia.

MRS ELLIOT: I'll find it. [*Goes to cocktail cabinet.*]

GEORGE: Cast of thousands, ten years in the making. Starring the one and only Mrs Elliot as Juno!

[*They all laugh with the exception of* PERCY. RUTH *comes in at the front door and stands listening at the foot of the stairs.*]

GEORGE [*assuming a thick Dublin accent*]: And you, Norah, me darlin', you shall play Ariadne.

NORAH: I'm not being a man for you or nobody.

GEORGE: And Josie, let me see, yes you'll play Semele.

JOSIE: Oh! There's a name to go to bed with!

GEORGE: And that's exactly what you do my sweet – with me, Jupiter.

[*More general laughter.* RUTH *goes upstairs.*]

PERCY: Accch!

MRS ELLIOT: There you are, Josie, what was I saying only a minute ago? [*Handing* GEORGE *corkscrew.*]

GEORGE: Now let the wine flow on this day of days. And what a day it's been. Do you know, one agent I went to see this morning looked me up and down in this duffel-coat and said: 'No, we ain't got no *Biblical* parts today.' Must have thought I looked like John the Baptist. Perhaps if I go in a kilt, he'll offer me a gangster part.

Glasses, Mrs E. Bring out the golden goblets. That's right. For in spite of George continually being told he's too young, too old, too short – in spite of his wig, glass eye, false teeth, and wooden leg, George has got himself a job. [*He hands wine to* MRS ELLIOT.] There we are.

MRS ELLIOT: I mustn't have more than one. I can't go to the meeting tiddly, can I? I don't know what Mr Colwyn-Stuart would say.

GEORGE: Josie?

JOSIE: I certainly won't say no. [*Takes glass.*]

GEORGE: And what about you, Percy. Will you have a tipple?

PERCY: Well, seeing as how you are in the money.

GEORGE: And Norah! A glass for Norah Mavourneen – me darlin' gal.

NORAH: Not for me, thank you.

GEORGE: No?

NORAH: No, thank you.

MRS ELLIOT: Oh, go on, Norah. It's no use you pretending you're teetotal. You had some on Boxing Day, I remember. Go on, be sociable.

NORAH: I really don't think I could after seeing those great fat men on the telly last night trampling on the grapes half naked. It was horrible.

GEORGE: So Norah isn't going to touch any more wine until they bath in a respectable manner? Never mind, dear, just one sip won't hurt you. [*Gives her a glass.*]

NORAH: Oh, all right then, just a sip.

MRS ELLIOT: Well, good health, George, and congratulations.

ALL: Good luck. Down the hatch, *etc.*

JOSIE: Well, now tell us what it is.

GEORGE: First of all, there's every chance of my play going on at the Trident Theatre.

MRS ELLIOT: Oh, good.

JOSIE: Where's that, George? In the West End?

GEORGE: Well, no, not exactly. Bayswater. And it means I should get plenty of managers and agents to see it.

MRS ELLIOT: Oh, good.

GEORGE: I saw Ronnie Harris this morning – you know the film man – and he said he's got a part for me coming up shortly.

NORAH: What sort of film, George?

GEORGE: Don't really know yet – to do with some Army job or something, so he says.

MRS ELLIOT: That'll be nice.

GEORGE: And finally, I've got a T.V. job coming up in three weeks' time.

JOSIE: George! You going to be on the telly?

GEORGE: Well, yes. But it's not exactly the lead, mind you, but it's something, anyway.

JOSIE: Oh, I'll say it is. Our George on the telly! What are you going to be in, George?

GEORGE: Ever heard of a play called *Hamlet*?

JOSIE: Of course I have.

NORAH: Yes, I saw that a long time ago. That's a very *old* one, isn't it. Very good though. He dies in the end, doesn't he?

GEORGE: He does indeed, Norah, he does.

NORAH: I always like a good laugh really. What I always say is –

NORAH: } There's enough misery in the world without paying to
GEORGE: } see it.

GEORGE: I don't think you really like the theatre very much, do you, Norah?

NORAH: Oh, yes I do.

GEORGE: Not really.

NORAH: Yes, but I don't ever go.

GEORGE: Oh, but you should. The theatre is like a shrine, Norah. A cathedral. Do you ever go to church, Norah?

MRS ELLIOT: The only time she goes to church is when she's got a blessed banner stuck in her hand.

NORAH: Oh, Mum. [*Rises and goes into lounge.*]

MRS ELLIOT: And talking of church – I must pop your Saviar in the oven. You'll be able to look after it, won't you? I'm off to the meeting as soon as Mr Colwyn-Stuart gets here. [*Exit kitchen.*]

GEORGE: Lord, is he coming? I'm in no mood for Mr Colwyn-pussy-Stuart. Josie, how long will you be?

JOSIE: How long will I be? Oooooh! It's jazz night! I must get changed. [*She runs upstairs.*]

GEORGE [*sinking exhausted in arm-chair*]: Tired as I am, anything would be better than having to put up with that moron.

PERCY: For once, young man, I agree with you. Thanks for the drink.

GEORGE [*absently*]: Not at all. A pleasure.

PERCY: Now that you're a celebrity, I'm surprised that you want to go jazzing at the Jubilee Hall with Josie.

GEORGE [*singing*]: 'Jazzing at the Jubilee with Josie!'

PERCY: And I certainly hope that now you are earning money, you will be able to pay for yourself instead of sponging off other people.

GEORGE [*looks at him sharply*]: What do you mean?

[*The front doorbell rings.*]

MRS ELLIOT [*in from kitchen*]: That's him now. Right on the dot as usual. Do I look all right?

[*RUTH comes downstairs.*]

GEORGE: Ravishing.

PERCY: Accch!

MRS ELLIOT [*into hall*]: Answer that, Ruth dear, will you? [*Into sitting room*] And if you can't make an effort to make yourself a little more pleasant, you'd better go and watch the telly.

PERCY [*sitting down*]: I'm busy.

[*RUTH opens front door.*]

MRS ELLIOT: All right then. But I don't want any upsets tonight. [*GEOFFREY COLWYN-STUART comes in and follows RUTH into sitting room. He wears an elegant suit, with a beautifully laundered shirt, a carefully chosen green spotted tie, and breast-pocket handkerchief to match. He is a pale, balding man in his late thirties, all sweetness and light.*]

MRS ELLIOT: Oh, come in Mr Stuart, I'm nearly ready. You know everyone don't you?

GEOFFREY: Yes, Good evening everyone. Why, Mrs Elliot, you look blooming tonight.

MRS ELLIOT: Oh, not really. I haven't had a minute since I came in.

GEOFFREY: But that's the secret, isn't it? Good evening Mr Elliot. How are you?

PERCY [*half rises, turning to greet Geoffrey but finally doesn't*]: How are you?

MRS ELLIOT: You've met George, haven't you?

GEOFFREY: Oh, yes, we've met several times, haven't we?

MRS ELLIOT: Yes. He's been here a long time now.

GEOFFREY: Like one of the family, in fact.

MRS ELLIOT: Well, I won't keep you long. I'll just pop upstairs and put on a spot of powder, then I'm ready. George'll keep you entertained. He keeps *us* entertained, doesn't he?

[PERCY *makes a noise like an aborted whistle, which he keeps up for the next few minutes,* RUTH *sits at the table, drinking tea.*]

MRS ELLIOT: Didn't you want to watch the television, Percy? George has had some good news today, haven't you, George? We've been ever so excited. He's going to be on the telly himself soon. You'll have to come round and see him when he is. I expect he'll tell you all about it. Make Mr Colwyn-Stuart comfortable. Don't go without me, now! [*Into hall and upstairs.*]

GEOFFREY: It's all right, you needn't hurry. We're early yet. [*Crossing left.*] What a dear she is.

GEORGE: Rather.

GEOFFREY: Mind if I sit here? [*At table.*]

RUTH: Do. There's some tea left, if you'd care for some.

GEOFFREY: No, thank you so much. I've just had dinner.

RUTH: Have you? We've just had supper. [*Removes wine to cocktail cabinet.*]

[PERCY *taps the sides of his arm-chair pensively.*]

GEOFFREY: And how's the world treating you, Mr Elliot? I suppose

I should say 'how are *you* treating the world?' After all, that's what really counts, isn't it?

PERCY: Not too badly, thank you.

GEOFFREY: Your wife's been telling me that you've not been sleeping very well lately. I'm sorry to hear that.

PERCY [*rubbing his nose*]: Oh? She told you that, did she?

GEOFFREY: She mentioned it at our last meeting actually.

PERCY: The last meeting was it? Actually?

GEOFFREY: How are you feeling now? Any better?

PERCY: Nothing the matter with me. Don't sleep so good sometimes, that's all.

GEOFFREY: Mrs Elliot says she can't persuade you to go to a doctor about it.

PERCY: Don't believe in them.

GEOFFREY: Well, I think you'll find plenty of people to support you there – including you, eh, George?

GEORGE: Right.

PERCY: I don't believe in a lot of vegetarian rot either. I'm not making *myself* ill. Meatless steaks! [*Grins.*]

RUTH: Yes, I must say, that was rather too much for me. Nut cutlet I can take, but meatless steak's a bit too much of a paradox. Do you think Oscar Wilde could possibly have been a vegetarian?

PERCY: It's just that I have a lot of things on my mind.

GEOFFREY: In your own words, Mr Elliot. Exactly. The old ravelled sleave of care, am I right, George?

GEORGE [*absently*]: Eh?

RUTH: Shakespeare, George. Aren't you supposed to stand to attention, or something?

GEOFFREY: The number of people one sees every day, with tired, haggard eyes, dark circles of care underneath them.

GEORGE: I always thought that had another significance.

GEOFFREY [*smiling*]: You're a pretty free sort of chap, aren't you? I hope you don't shock everyone in this respectable household with your Bohemian ways.

GEORGE: By 'Bohemian' I suppose you mean crummy. It's rather like calling bad breath 'halitosis', don't you think?

RUTH: He's straight out of *Trilby* – didn't you know?

GEORGE: Frankly, I always touch mine up with a brown liner.

GEOFFREY: What?

GEORGE: The rings under my eyes – helps me when I play clergymen's parts. I'm rather good at them.

GEOFFREY [*refusing to be stung*]: You know, you surprise me a little, George. You seem such an intelligent, vital young man, so much in the swim. After all, it's not even considered fashionable to be sceptical nowadays. The really *smart* thing is the spiritual thing.

RUTH: That's true enough.

GEOFFREY: And you too, Ruth. Of course, your interests are political, I know. But shall I tell you something? If I were to invite the Foreign Secretary, say, down here to speak, he wouldn't be able to half fill the Jubilee Hall.

RUTH: Are we supposed to be surprised?

GEOFFREY: On the other hand, if I were to invite someone like Billy Graham – well, take my word for it, you wouldn't be able to get within a mile of the place.

RUTH: With his message of love and all that? Love isn't everything, you know, Mr Stuart.

GEOFFREY: That's where we disagree, Ruth. I believe that it is.

RUTH: Take justice away from love, and it doesn't mean a thing.

GEOFFREY: Love can change the face of the world.

RUTH: Tell that to the poor black devils in South Africa. Why don't you do something for them?

GEOFFREY: Dear, oh dear – we're going to get involved already if we're not careful. I can see that. Oh, there's nothing I enjoy more than a good old intellectual rough and tumble, and I only wish I could stay and slog it out with the two of you, but there isn't time, unfortunately. The fact is, we've probably got a great deal in common. You know: I have discovered a new way of judging people.

RUTH: You have?

GEOFFREY: I simply ask myself whether their lights are shining.

GEORGE: What about their livers?

GEOFFREY [*laughing*]: Yes. I did phrase it badly didn't I? Perhaps I should have said 'lamps'. I ask myself whether their lamps are shining. You see, my theory is that inside every one of us is a lamp. When it's alight, the loves and hates, the ambitions, desires, and ideas inside it are burning, and that person is really alive. But there are people who go around every day, at work, at home with their families – they seem normal, but their lamps have gone out. They've simply given up. They've given up being alive.

RUTH: And are our lamps alight, do you think, Mr Stuart?

GEOFFREY: Oh, very definitely. It struck me the moment I came into the room.

GEORGE: Tell me. [*Nodding at Percy.*] What about Mr Elliot's lamp?

GEOFFREY: Oh, yes, I think so. I think so. It's burning all right.

GEORGE: You *think* so! You hear that, Percy? You need a new wick.

GEOFFREY: Oh, I hope I didn't sound rude. I think Mr Elliot is on edge about things a little perhaps, principally because he's tired and can't sleep.

PERCY: All I said was –

GEOFFREY: People are wearing themselves out, worrying about a whole lot of things, unimportant things that don't matter one jot. You, Ruth, you worry about who's going to win the next election.

RUTH: Believe me – I no longer give a *damn*.

GEOFFREY: It's not important. And you, George, you worry about whether you're going to rise to the top of your profession. That's not important.

GEORGE: Thank you. We'll let you know.

GEOFFREY: One day – a few years ago this was – I happened to speak to a very famous clergyman – oh, he's dead now –

PERCY: He's all right then.

GEOFFREY: For years that man was in the habit of addressing as

43

many as six different meetings in one day, often in the same number of towns. So I asked him how it was that he never seemed to get even a little bit tired. And he explained it to me. He said: 'Because I believe in every single word that I utter.'

GEORGE: Lucky him.

GEOFFREY: You could see his lamp burning at the very back of the hall. He was on fire for what he believed in. And that's the secret. It's no use sitting around moaning.

[*Enter* MRS ELLIOT *from hall.*]

MRS ELLIOT: Who's been moaning? I'm all ready. The television's started, Percy. Have you been having a little chat with George?

GEOFFREY: Well, not exactly. I'm afraid I've been rather bad mannered.

MRS ELLIOT: I'm quite sure you haven't. *You're* never bad mannered with anyone.

GEOFFREY: I have been rather monopolizing the conversation. In fact, I've a teeny-weeny feeling that George and Ruth think I'm rather an old bore.

MRS ELLIOT: Of course he doesn't. He's a very deep one, George – I know that.

GEOFFREY: What really started us off was – we were talking about tiredness. It's a long time since I heard *you* complaining of tiredness, Mrs Elliot. Not since those very early days just after – just after the end of the war. I think she's a good advertisement for the system, don't you? No doubt, it sounds a little odd to you, but it's all a question of what *we* call synchronizing yourself with Providence. Of getting into step with the almighty.

MRS ELLIOT: Yes. Well, I think we ought to be getting in step ourselves, Mr Stuart, don't you?

GEOFFREY: Yes, I suppose we had.

[*She turns to go, and* GEOFFREY *rises.* GEORGE *has hardly been listening, but suddenly he responds, almost as an afterthought to himself.*]

GEORGE: Yes. If only it were as simple as that, Mr Stuart. But life isn't simple, and, if you've any brains in your head at all, it's frankly a pain in the arse.

MRS ELLIOT: George! Really!

GEORGE: I'm sorry. I apologize. But I've said it now. You see, to me there is something contemptible about a man who can't face it all without drugging himself up to the rings round his eyes with a lot of comforting myths – like all these bird-brains who batten off the National Health. I don't care who it is – you or anyone – you must have a secret doubt somewhere. You know that the only reason you do believe in these things is because they *are* comforting.

GEOFFREY: So you think that religion is just a series of useful untruths?

GEORGE: Yes, I do.

PERCY: Hear! Hear!

MRS ELLIOT: You be quiet!

GEOFFREY: It's all right, Mrs Elliot. George is like so many young men – he believes that the great thing about the truth is that it must always be unpleasant.

GEORGE: It's just that I believe it's easy to answer the ultimate questions – it saves you bothering with the immediate ones.

MRS ELLIOT: There's such a thing as faith, George.

GEORGE: I believe in evidence. And faith is believing in something for which there *is* no evidence. You don't say: I have faith that two and two are four, do you? Or that the earth is round? And why? Because they're both easily verified.

GEOFFREY: So it all has to be verified for you, does it, George? I think I understand you better than you know.

GEORGE: Oh?

GEOFFREY: You see, I come into contact with a great many artistic people. What *do* you believe in? Yourself?

GEORGE: Right. [*Adding in vocal parenthesis*] He said, striking attitude of genius.

GEOFFREY: You have faith. You have faith in yourself – in your talent. Am I right?

GEORGE: Well?

GEOFFREY: Your talent, George. You believe in that with all your heart. And your evidence? Where is that, George? Can you show it to me?

[*Pause. They all look at him.*]

RUTH: *Touché.*

[GEORGE *is still for a moment. Then he laughs.*]

GEORGE: What a performance! All this Jesuit subtlety! You're too much for me. Just say that I'm like Christopher Columbus – I haven't discovered America yet. But it's there all right, waiting to be, yes, verified.

GEOFFREY: Yes, I'm quite sure it is. You see, I have faith too. I can see the lamp burning. Well, we really must be off. Come along, Mrs Elliot. Good night, everybody.

MRS ELLIOT: Yes. Well, I shan't be back late.

[*They both go into hall, and out through the front door.*]

PERCY [*rising and crossing to doorway*]: Lamps! [*Chuckling, turns.*] 'E ought to be on the bleeding stage – not you! [*Exit to lounge.*]

RUTH: Are you all right. You look a bit shaken.

GEORGE: I'm all right. I rather stupidly let the conducting of divine lip-service irritate me.

RUTH: So I noticed.

GEORGE: It's just been a pretty awful day, that's all.

RUTH: You surprise me.

GEORGE: Do I?

RUTH: Not really. You aren't very impressed with Geoffrey, I take it?

GEORGE: Right. What the Americans call 'strictly for the birds'. If there should be any heavenly purpose at all behind Mr Colwyn-phoney-Stuart, it's that he's God's own gift to the birds. Hope I didn't upset Mrs Elliot though. She's obviously pretty taken up with the whole racket.

RUTH: It might help if you weren't quite so vicious about it. You sound like a man with a secret doubt yourself.

GEORGE: Why is it you distrust me so much? I had a feeling we were the same kind.

RUTH: Did you? I suppose it's given poor Kate something to think about since Raymond was killed.

GEORGE: Tell me –

RUTH: Yes?

GEORGE: What was he really like?

RUTH: Raymond? Nice enough boy. Hard working, conscientious. Like most decent, ordinary lads of his age. [*Their eyes meet.*] You aren't remotely alike.

GEORGE: I thought you were in the habit of pitching into her yourself, hammer and sickle, over the Colwyn-Stuart.

RUTH: I should have thought that was different.

GEORGE: You mean that you're one of the family, and I'm not?

RUTH: If you like.

GEORGE: Suppose I'd better apologize.

RUTH: I shouldn't worry. I can't imagine what you could do wrong in her eyes. Well – I can imagine it all right, but I can't see you being stupid enough to lose the only good friend you've got.

GEORGE: What makes you think I haven't any good friends?

RUTH: Have you?

GEORGE: I thought you steel-hardened cadres of the far-away left had a better defence against the little jokies of right wing deviationists like me. Or is it Wall Street jackal? No – I don't really look much like a jackal. Villiers Street wolf perhaps.

RUTH: Very droll – but not very well timed for someone who is supposed to be an actor.

GEORGE: Join my fan club, won't you?

RUTH: I'm not in the right frame of mind for shoddy little gags. [*Pause.*] I looked up the Party secretary tonight.

GEORGE: So you've packed it in at last.

RUTH: No doubt you think it's pretty funny.

GEORGE: No. I don't think it's funny.

RUTH: Seventeen years. It's rather like walking out on a lover. All over, finished, kaput. He hardly listened to my explanation – just sat there with a sneer all over his face. He didn't even have the manners to get up and show me out. I think that's what I've hated most of all, all these years – the sheer, damned bad manners of the lot of them.

GEORGE: Farther left you go, the worse the manners seem to get.

RUTH: Well! The house is still fairly ringing with the bloody shovel of *your* opinions.

GEORGE: *I* have a sense of humour. 'Bloody shovel of your opinions!' Is that a quotation?

RUTH: Just someone I used to know. Someone rather like you, in fact.

GEORGE: I thought you'd tied me up with someone the moment I met you.

RUTH: Where are you going tonight?

GEORGE: Dancing, I believe. Somewhere Josie knows.

RUTH: Don't sound so apologetic about it. It doesn't suit you. Pass my handbag, will you?

[*He does so.*]

RUTH: Looks as though you've a long wait ahead of you, my lad. [*She offers him a cigarette.*]

GEORGE: Have one of mine. [*Fumbles in his pockets.*]

RUTH: You needn't go through the pantomime for me, George. Take one.

GEORGE: No thank you.

RUTH: Oh, don't look like that, for God's sake! You make me feel as though I'm – setting up as a soup kitchen or something. Please. [*She throws a cigarette. He catches it, fumbles for a light. She snaps a lighter at him, and he goes over to her. He bends over her for a light.*]

GEORGE: How young you look sometimes.

RUTH: So do you when you're silent, and no longer trying to justify yourself.

GEORGE: What's the time?

RUTH: Seven-fifteen. Where's your watch?

GEORGE: Being repaired.

RUTH: Pawned, I suppose.

GEORGE: Just as you like. I think I'll give Josie a yell.

RUTH: It won't do any good – not for ages yet. I didn't mean to hurt you just now.

GEORGE: Didn't you?

RUTH: Yes. You're quite right. I did mean to hurt you. I wish I hadn't.

GEORGE: What are you doing tonight?

RUTH: I don't know yet. I'm getting rather used to being at home every night. I *did* apologize.

GEORGE: We're neither of us as steel-hardened as we should be, are we? I used to smoke my mother's cigarettes too. Right up until the time she died.

RUTH: When was that?

GEORGE: Couple of years ago. We often used to go out together – she enjoyed that more than anything. She'd pay for the lot: drinks, meals, cinemas – even the bus fares. When the conductor came up the stairs, I would always grope in my pockets. And my mother would bring out her purse, and push my empty, fumbling hands away. 'It's all right, dear, I've got change.' I used to wonder whether perhaps there might come just *one* day when it might not have to happen. When I might actually have that two shillings or half-crown in my pocket. But it always did. It had become a liturgy. We went through it the last time we went out together – on my thirtieth birthday. During the war it was different. I was well paid then.

RUTH: What did he give you for it?

GEORGE: What?

RUTH: The pawnbroker – for the watch?

GEORGE: Fifteen shillings. I was lucky to get that – it wasn't a very good one.

RUTH: Here. [*Takes out Jock's watch from handbag, and holds it out to him.*] Well, take it.

GEORGE: What's this?

RUTH: What does it look like? Try it on.

GEORGE [*taking it*]: Are you giving me this?

RUTH: Yes, but you don't have to make a meal out of it.

GEORGE: It must have cost a fortune.

RUTH: It did. Try not to pawn it. Or, if you do, tell me, and I can renew the ticket or something.

GEORGE: I shan't pawn it, I promise you. I think it must be the nicest present I've had. How do you fix it?

RUTH: Here – [*She adjusts it for him, he watches her.*]

GEORGE: Your – friend?

RUTH: Oh, he doesn't want it any more. He told me.

GEORGE: Can you get the Third Programme on it?

RUTH: There!

GEORGE: Perhaps it'll change my luck.

RUTH: Superstitious too?

GEORGE: Thank you. Very much.

[*She still has his hand in hers.*]

RUTH: How beautiful your hands are – they're like marble, so white and clear.

GEORGE: Nonsense.

RUTH: But they are. I've never seen such beautiful hands.

GEORGE: You make it sound as if I were half dead already.

[*She looks up quickly, disturbed. Quite suddenly, he kisses her. Almost as quickly, he releases her. She soon recovers and moves away.*]

RUTH: Did you notice what I did with my lighter? My cigarette's gone out.

GEORGE: Didn't you put it back in your bag?

[*She opens it.*]

RUTH: So I did. What sort of parts do you play? On the stage, I mean.

GEORGE: Good ones.

RUTH: Stupid question deserves a stupid answer. I mean: any particular type.

GEORGE: I suppose so. Reminds me of the actor who was asked at an audition what sort of parts he played, and he replied, 'Scornful parts.' I think I play 'scornful' parts – anyone a bit loud-mouthed, around my height, preferably rough and dirty, with a furnace roaring in his belly. The rougher and dirtier the better.

RUTH: A character actor in fact.

GEORGE: I'm sorry I kissed you. So you needn't try to pay me back for it.

RUTH: Don't apologize. I was flattered for a moment. I'm sure there's an explanation somewhere, but I'd rather you didn't try to tell me what it is.

GEORGE: Just as you like.

RUTH: First time I've tasted Brown Windsor.

GEORGE: Tasted what?

RUTH [*laughing*]: The Brown Windsor of love, George. Haven't you come across it.

GEORGE: That – friend of yours sounds rather pretentious to me.

RUTH: It's funny how rhetorical gentle spirits can become.

GEORGE: He's a poet or something?

RUTH: I used to hope so.

[GEORGE *stretches himself.*]

GEORGE: God, I feel tired!

[*He looks all round the room. His eyes rest on Raymond's painted birds on the back wall, centre.*]

Blimey! Those birds! [*Goes upstage and walks around and is finally stopped by the sight of the cocktail cabinet.*] I've sat here for weeks now and looked at that. Oh, I've often marvelled at them from afar in a shop window. But I never thought I'd ever see one in someone's house. I thought they just stood there, in a pool of neon, like some sort of monstrous symbol, surrounded by bilious dining-room suites and mattresses and things. It never occurred to me that anyone bought them!

RUTH: Norah's cocktail cabinet? Well, she didn't actually buy it – she won it.

GEORGE: What was her reaction?

RUTH: I think we were all a little over-awed by it.

[GEORGE *goes nearer to it.*]

GEORGE: It looks as though it has come out of a jelly-mould like an American car. What do you suppose you *do* with it? You don't keep drinks in it – that's just a front, concealing its true mystery. What do you keep in it – old razor blades? I know, I've got it!

[*He sits down and 'plays' it vigorously, like a cinema organ, humming a 'lullaby-lane' style signature tune. He turns a beaming face to Ruth.*]

And now I'm going to finish up with a short selection of popular symphonies, entitled 'Evergreens from the Greats', ending up with Beethoven's Ninth! And don't forget – if you're enjoying yourself, then all join in. If you can't remember the words, let alone understand 'em, well, just whistle the tune. Here we go then!

[*Encouraged by* RUTH'S *laughter, he turns back and crashes away on the cocktail cabinet, pulling out the stops and singing:*]

> 'I fell in love with ye-ieuw!
> While we were dancing
> The Beethoven Waltz! . . .'

A final flourish on the invisible keyboard; he turns and bows obsequiously. RUTH'S *response has exhilarated him, and he stands in front of her, rather flushed.*]

It ought to disappear somehow, but I couldn't find the combination. [*He watches her with pleasure.*] That's the first time you've ever laughed.

RUTH: Oh, yes, you can be funny, George. These flashes of frenzy, the torrents of ideas, they can be quite funny, even exciting at times. If I don't laugh, it's because I know I shall see fatigue and fear in your eyes sooner or later.

GEORGE: Oh?

RUTH: You're burning yourself out. And for what?

GEORGE: Go on – but don't think you can kill my confidence. I've had experts doing it for years.

RUTH: I just can't make up my mind about you.

GEORGE: Meaning?

RUTH: Do you really have any integrity?

GEORGE: What's *your* verdict?

RUTH: I'm still not sure. It just seems to me that for someone who makes a religion out of being brilliant, you must be very unlucky.

GEORGE: You don't even begin to understand – you're no different from the rest. Burning myself out! You bet I'm burning myself out! I've been doing it for so many years now – and who in hell cares? At this moment I feel about as empty and as threadbare as my pockets. You wonder that I should be tired. I feel played out.

[*She applauds.*]

RUTH: Bravo! Not bad at all, George. Bit ragged maybe, but it'll do. Perhaps you may not be so bad after all. Tell me about this television job.

GEORGE: That? It's a walk-on – one line which will be drowned by the rest anyway. And if I know Lime Grove, it'll be so dark, I shan't be seen at all. All for twelve guineas. It's a fortune. But what am I going to do? How can I let them all sit there – and probably half the street as well – staring stupidly at the telly for two and a half hours to watch me make one thirty-second appearance at the very end? What a triumph for dear old Percy! And Mr Colwyn-Stuart and his Hallelujah Chorus!

RUTH: Quite a problem.

GEORGE: As it is, I owe Mrs Elliot God-knows how much. But I suppose you knew that.

RUTH: It's not exactly a surprise.

GEORGE: She was buying me cigarettes every day up until last week. I did manage to put a stop to that. I told her I was giving it up for my health. To my surprise, she actually believed me.

RUTH: *Are* you any good, George?

GEORGE [*almost like a child*]: That's a moron's question.

RUTH: As you like.

GEORGE: Well, ask yourself. Isn't it? Listen: all I ever got – inside and outside the theatre – is the raves of a microscopic minority, and the open hostility of the rest. I attract hostility. I seem to be on heat for it. Whenever I step out on to those boards – immediately, from the very first moment I show my face – I know I've got to fight almost every one of those people in the auditorium. Right from the stalls to the gallery, to the Vestal Virgins in the boxes! My God, it's a gladiatorial combat! Me against Them! Me and mighty Them! Oh, I may win some of them over. Sometimes it's a half maybe, sometimes a third, sometimes, it's not even a quarter. But I *do* beat them down. I beat them down! And even in the hatred of the majority, there's a kind of triumph because I know that, although they'd never admit it, they secretly respect me.

RUTH: What about this film you're going to be in?

GEORGE: It doesn't mean a thing. The old line. You know? Keep in touch – we'll let you know. You *don't* understand, do you?

RUTH: I just don't see much virtue in trying to ignore failure.

GEORGE: There's no such thing as failure – just waiting for success.

RUTH: George – really!

GEORGE: All right, forget it.

RUTH: I know what it is to go on waiting.

GEORGE: And do you think I don't! I spend my life next to a telephone. Every time it rings is like death to me.

RUTH [*relentless*]: What about these plays you write? You do do that as well, don't you?

GEORGE: Oh yes – you think I'm a dabbler. A dilettante who can't afford it.

RUTH: This Trident Theatre – the 'three uplifted fingers of Drama, Ballet, and Poetry –'

GEORGE: A so-called club theatre, meaning a preciously over-decorated flea-pit, principally famous for its rather tarty bar, and frequented almost exclusively by intense students, incompetent longhairs, and rather flashy deadbeats generally.

RUTH: I see. I'd like to read some of your work.

GEORGE: Thank you, I'll think about it.

RUTH: Do you charge a fee?

54

GEORGE: You're not being very funny yourself now.

RUTH: Perhaps your sense of humour has deserted you after all. My politics and your art – they seem to be like Kate's religion, better not discussed. Rationally, at any rate.

GEORGE: I knew you were suspicious of me, that you distrusted me. I didn't realize you detested me this much.

RUTH: George: why don't you go?

GEORGE: Go?

RUTH: Leave this house. Get out of here. If you're what you believe yourself to be, you've no place in a house like this. It's unfair to you. It's stifling. You should be with your own kind. And if you're not what you say you are, you've no right to be here anyway, and you're being unfair to everyone.

GEORGE: Are you serious? I haven't got a penny in the world.

RUTH: You'll manage. You've got to. It's your only chance of survival. Am I being harsh, George? Perhaps, as you say, we're the same kind.

GEORGE [savagely]: That's good! Oh yes! And what about you?

RUTH [off her balance]: What about me?

GEORGE: What are you doing here? All right, you've had your go at me. But what about yourself?

RUTH: Well?

GEORGE: Oh, don't be so innocent, Ruth. This house! This room! This hideous, God-awful room!

RUTH: Aren't you being just a little insulting?

GEORGE: I'm simply telling you what you very well know. They may be your relations, but have you honestly got one tiny thing in common with any of them? These people –

RUTH: Oh, no! Not 'these people'! Please – not that! After all, they don't still keep coals in the bath.

GEORGE: I didn't notice. Have you looked at them? Have you listened to them? They don't merely act and talk like caricatures, they are caricatures! That's what's so terrifying. Put any one of them on a stage, and no one would take them seriously for one minute! They think in clichés, they talk in them, they even feel in them – and, brother, that's an achievement! Their existence is one great cliché that they carry about with them like a snail in his little house – and they live in it and die in it!

RUTH: Even if it's true – and I don't say it is – you still sound pretty cheap saying it.

GEORGE: Look at that wedding group. [*Points to it.*] Look at it! It's like a million other grisly groups – all tinted in unbelievable pastels; round-shouldered girls with crinkled-up hair, open mouths, and bad teeth. The bridegroom looks as gormless as he's feeling lecherous, and the bride – the bride's looking as though she's just been thrown out of an orgy at a Druids' reunion! Mr and Mrs Elliot at their wedding. It stands there like a comic monument to the macabre farce that has gone on between them in this house ever since that greatest day in a girl's life thirty-five years ago.

RUTH: Oh, a good delivery, George. You're being brilliant, after all. They're very easy people to score off, but, never mind, go on!

GEORGE: There's Josie – at this moment putting all she's got into misapplying half Woolworth's on to her empty, characterless little face. Oh, sneer at me for my snobbery, for my bad taste, but, say what you like: I have a mind and feelings that are all fingertips. Josie's mind. She can hardly spell it. And her feelings – what about them? All thumbs, thumbs that are fat and squashy – like bananas, in fact, and rather sickly.

RUTH: You should look an intriguing couple on the dance floor tonight. I'm tempted to come myself.

GEORGE: Why don't you?

RUTH: I should hate to break up this marriage of true minds.

GEORGE: You know damned well why I'm going. People like me depend upon the Josies of this world. The great, gaping mass that you're so fond of. You know? And for tonight, Josie is that mass, all rolled into one. And do you know what? Behind that brooding cloud of mascara, she's got her eye on George, Josie has. Because not only does she suffer from constipation, but night starvation as well. And then, there's Norah. Now what can you say about her? Norah doesn't even exist – she's just a hole in the air!

RUTH: You've a lot to learn yet, George. If there weren't people like the Elliots, people like you couldn't exist. Don't forget that. Don't think it's the other way around, because it's not. They can do without you, take my word for it. But without them, you're lost – nothing.

GEORGE: Don't give me that, Ruth. They drive you mad, and you know it. It's like living in one of those really bad suitable-for-all-the-family comedies they do all the year round in weekly rep. in Wigan. How have you stuck it here? What's the secret? Tell me. Since that mysterious divorce of yours that they all heavy-handedly avoid mentioning – and the week-end trips you don't make any more. How long is it you've been here? How long? Nine years is it? Ten years? Twelve? On no, Ruth – *you* can't afford to sneer at me!

RUTH: You've made your point. Don't get carried away with it. Why do I stay? Because I don't earn enough to get me out of it, and somewhere else. I spend too much on clothes, cigarettes –

GEORGE: And – 'incidentals'? [*Holding up wrist-watch.*]

RUTH: The job I do is so hysterically dull that every time I go into that office, and see myself surrounded by those imitation human beings, I feel so trapped and helpless that I could yell my lungs out with the loneliness and the boredom of it.

GEORGE: So you do!

RUTH: But, at my age, and with my lack of the right kind of qualifications, there's not much else I can do. Perhaps I haven't the courage to try. At least, I'm safe. And so I go on, from spring, through the summer, to the autumn and another winter, meaningless; just another caricature.

GEORGE: I knew it! I knew it!

RUTH: Thank you for reminding me of it.

GEORGE: The truth is a caricature.

RUTH: Is that meant to be profound?

GEORGE: You hate them, don't you? Shall I tell you why they horrify me?

RUTH: I suppose I give you what is known as the 'feed' line now. No – tell me, why do they horrify you?

GEORGE: They've no curiosity. There are no questions for them, and, consequently, no answers. They've no apprehension, no humility –

RUTH: Humility! [*Laughing.*] Good old George!

GEORGE: And, above all, no real laughter. Tell me, have you ever heard any of them, even once, laugh? I mean really laugh – not make that choked, edgy sound that people make all the time. Or, to put it more unintelligibly: I don't mean that breaking wind people make somewhere between their eyebrows and their navels, when they hear about the old lady's most embarrassing moment. I mean the real thing – the sound of the very wit of being alive. Laughter's the nearest we ever get, or should get, to sainthood. It's the state of grace that saves most of us from contempt.

RUTH: Hooray!

GEORGE: No, it wasn't really spontaneous. Singing and dancing 'Jazzing at the Jubilee with Josie'.

RUTH: Why haven't we talked like this before? A few moments ago you made me feel old. Now, I suddenly feel younger.

GEORGE: 'If you can't give a dollar, give me a lousy dime . . .'

RUTH: Can't say I've exactly heard *you* falling about with mirth since you came here.

GEORGE: No, you haven't. I suppose it does sound as though I'm complaining because everyone doesn't go round as if they were on parole from *Crime and Punishment*, muttering about God, and laughing their blooming heads off.

RUTH: Oh yes, you are a character! I think your little performance has done me good.

GEORGE: You're a good audience. Even if I do have to beat you down. That's all I need – an audience.

RUTH: And do you – think you'll find it?

GEORGE: I don't know.

[*He takes a deep breath, and sits down quickly, suddenly drained. She watches him, fascinated.*]

RUTH: How quickly you change! That's what's so frightening about you. These agonizing bubbles of personality, then phut! Nothing. Simply tiredness and pain.

GEORGE: I've been trailing around all day. I've had a few drinks, and nothing to eat. It suddenly hit me, that's all.

RUTH: Perhaps you have got talent, George. I don't know. Who can tell? Even the experts can't always recognize it when they see it. You may even be great. But don't make a disease out of it. You're sick with it.

GEORGE: It's a disease some of us long to have.

RUTH: I know that. I met it once before.

GEORGE: Then you must know it's incurable.

RUTH: Galloping – like a consumption.

GEORGE [*sharply*]: What did that mean?

RUTH: Nothing.

GEORGE: But do you know what is worse? Far, far worse?

RUTH: No, Brother Bones, tell me what is worse.

GEORGE: What is worse is having the same symptoms as talent, the pain, the ugly swellings, the lot – but never knowing whether or not the diagnosis is correct. Do you think there may be some kind of euthanasia for that? Could you kill it by burying yourself here – for good?

RUTH: Why do you ask me?

GEORGE: Would the warm, generous, honest-to-goodness animal lying at your side every night, with its honest-to-goodness love – would it make you forget?

RUTH: All you're saying is that it's a hard world to live in if you're a poet – particularly if it should happen that you're not a very good poet.

GEORGE: Unquote.

RUTH: Unquote. Life is hard, George. Anyone who thinks it isn't is either very young or a fool. And you're not either. Perhaps even bad artists have their place in the scheme of things.

GEORGE: Scheme of flaming things! Get us with our intellectual sets on! And we're not even tight. I wish we were spending the evening together, all the same.

RUTH: Why are you so morbidly self-conscious? I thought all actors revelled in exhibitionism.

GEORGE: Don't you believe it. Only insincere old bastards who carried spears with Martin Harvey, and have been choking themselves silly with emotion ever since. 'Emotion, laddie – that's the secret!' Shall I tell you a story? Yes, do tell me a story. Well, it happened to me when I was in the R.A.F. during the war.

RUTH: I didn't know you were. You've never mentioned it.

GEORGE: The one thing I never shoot lines about is the R.A.F. Just a gap in my life. That's all. Well, it happened like this: It was one night in particular, when it wasn't my turn to go on ops. Instead, we got a basinful of what we gave the Jerries, smack bang in the middle of the camp. I remember flinging myself down, not so much on to the earth as into it. A wing commander type pitched himself next to me, and, together, we shared his tin-helmet. Fear ran through the whole of my body, the strange fear that my right leg would be blown off, and how terrible it would be. Suddenly the winco shouted at me above the din: 'What's your profession?' 'Actor,' I said. The moment I uttered that word, machine-gun fire and bombs all around us, the name of my calling, my whole reason for existence – it sounded so hideously trivial and unimportant, so divorced from living, and the real world, that my fear vanished. All I could feel was shame.

[*He is lost for a moment or two. Then he looks at her quickly, and adds brightly.*]

Gifted people are always dramatizing themselves. It provides its own experience, I suppose.

RUTH: How pompous can you get? You had me under your spell for a moment. Now you've broken it. I'm beginning not to know when you're being real, and when you're not.

GEORGE: Always put the gun in the other man's hand. It's my rule of life.

RUTH: Yes. You're play acting all right. You've done it all your life, and you'll go on doing it. You can't tell what's real and what isn't any more, can you, George? I can't sit here drivelling all night.
[*She turns to go.*]

GEORGE [*taking her by the arm*]: And what if I do? What does it matter? My motives aren't as simple as you like to think –

RUTH: – You're being phoney, George, aren't you? We're a pair of –

GEORGE: – What if I am? Or you, for that matter? It's just as –

RUTH [*sings*]: 'It's a Barnum and Bailey world,
　　　　　　Just as phoney as it can be!'
You've got us both acting it now –

GEORGE: – just as serious and as complex as any other attitude. Ruth! Believe me, it isn't any less –

RUTH: – haven't you, George? Cutting in on each other's lives –

GEORGE: – real or sincere. You just never stop standing outside –

RUTH: – fluffing your emotions –

GEORGE: – it's a penance –

RUTH: – that's the word, isn't it? You're fluffing it –

GEORGE: – the actor's second sense –

RUTH: – all studied, premeditated –

GEORGE: – watching, observing, watching me now, commenting, analysing, giggling –

RUTH: – timed for effect, deliberate, suspect –

GEORGE: – just at this moment, don't you want me more than anything else –

RUTH: I've had my lot, George.

GEORGE: More than anything?

RUTH: We've both had our lots!

GEORGE: You're as arrogant as I am!

RUTH: You know what, George?

GEORGE: That's one of the reasons you're drawn to me! If only you knew – how much – at this moment –

RUTH: No, not me. Somebody else – not me!

GEORGE: I mean it, damn you!

RUTH: Strictly for the birds, George! Strictly for the birds!

GEORGE: Ruth!

RUTH: Let me go!

[*He does so.*]

GEORGE [*simply*]: I've botched it. [*Pause.*] Haven't I?

[*The descent has been so sudden, and they are both dazed.*]

RUTH: I'm not sure what has happened. Nothing I suppose. We're just two rather lost people – nothing extraordinary. Anyway, I'm past the stage for casual affairs. [*Turns away.*] You can't go on being Bohemian at forty.

[JOSIE *comes running down the stairs into the sitting room. She is wearing her 'jazz trousers'.*]

JOSIE: Ready?

GEORGE: Yes. Yes, I suppose so.

[RUTH *goes quickly out through the french windows.*]

JOSIE: Well, come on then. Had your supper?

GEORGE: No. I don't want anything. Let's have a drink, shall we, before we go?

JOSIE: Oh yes, lovely!

[GEORGE *does not move.*]

Well, what are you standing there for? What are you thinking about?

GEORGE: What am I thinking about? [*To cocktail cabinet for the wine.*] What am I thinking about? [*Pouring drinks*] Do you realize, Josie, that that is a lover's question? 'What are you thinking about?' [*Hands her a drink.*]

JOSIE: Oh, you are daft. You make me laugh when you talk in riddles. Oh, well, cheers!

GEORGE: Cheers. It'll be tonight, Josephine. [*Drinks.*]

JOSIE: Whatever are you talking about? You are in a funny mood, I must say. Let's have some music while we finish our drinks. [*She goes to radiogram.*] We don't want to get there too early, do we?

GEORGE: All the best people arrive late.

JOSIE [*looking through records*]: What shall we have? There's 'Mambo Man', 'Jambo Mambo', or 'Marmalade Mambo'.

GEORGE: Oh, let's have something to soothe my rather shabby soul, Josie.

JOSIE: Go on, you haven't got one. What about this then?
[*She puts on Mantovani.*]

GEORGE [*screwing up his face*]: Heaven. [*They begin dancing.*] Sheer heaven.
[*After a moment.*]

JOSIE: Bit boring isn't it – the music I mean.

GEORGE: The preliminaries always are, Josie, my girl. But they make anticipation all the more exciting. Are you ever excited by anticipation?

JOSIE: No, not really. Only when I see fellows like Len Cook, he's lovely.

GEORGE: That's not anticipation, Josie, that's lust, plain lust. Although it never is really plain. Do you know what lust is, Josie?

JOSIE: Of course I do, silly.

GEORGE: Lust, the harshest detergent of them all, the expense of spirit in a waste of shame. Or as Jean Paul Sartre put it – sex.

JOSIE: We were only talking about sex a little while ago. Boring, I think.

GEORGE: Do you? Shall we go?

JOSIE: All right.
[*They move into the hall. At the foot of the stairs,* GEORGE *stops her.*]

GEORGE: Have you ever been kissed, Josie?

JOSIE: Hundreds of times.

GEORGE: Like this?
[*He kisses her fiercely. The lounge door opens and they do not see* PERCY *standing there.* RUTH *comes in through french windows, switches out main lights, leaving just a glow in the sitting room.* PERCY *remains silhouetted against the light from the lounge as* RUTH *sits in arm-chair.*]

JOSIE: George – don't George, there's somebody coming!

GEORGE: I've never tried the etchings line – [*leading her up the stairs*] – let's see if it really works.

JOSIE: But George –

GEORGE: Come and see my etchings. [*They are by now halfway upstairs.*]

JOSIE: What are you –

[GEORGE *smothers her with another kiss.*]

GEORGE: Silly girl.

JOSIE: But, George, what will Mum say?

[*They are swallowed up in darkness.* PERCY *moves towards the foot of the stairs and looks up. Then he moves into the sitting room and looks down at* RUTH *for a moment. She is suddenly aware of him.*]

RUTH: Why, Percy, how long have you been there?

PERCY: Long enough, I think. Quite long enough.

QUICK CURTAIN

ACT THREE

SCENE 1

Autumn.

[*One french window is open.* GEORGE *is lying on the settee in his shirt sleeves. His jacket is hung on the back of one of the chairs. There are some loose leaves of manuscript scattered by the side of the settee. After a moment,* GEORGE *shivers, gets up, and puts on his jacket.* MRS ELLIOT *comes downstairs into the sitting room with a breakfast tray.*]

MRS ELLIOT: Are you feeling any better, dear. You need not have got up at all, you know. [*She puts tray on table.*] Silly boy – the window open too. [*Crossing to window.*] You'll catch your death. The chrysanths have gone off. Chrysanths always remind me of Father. [*Stands at the window. Shuts it.*] Oh, dear, the clocks go back tonight. Awful, isn't it? [*Picks up tray.*] You didn't eat much breakfast, dear. [*Into kitchen.*] Your bed's made and your room is done if you want to go up any time. Nearly twelve – [*in from the kitchen*] the others will be back soon. Sure you're all right dear? Everyone's a bit down in the dumps these days. It must be the winter coming on. Not that I mind it really. It's the awful in-between that gets me down. How's the writing going? All right?

GEORGE: Oh, not too bad, Mrs Elliot, thanks. Feeling a bit whacked at the moment though.

MRS ELLIOT: Well, you mustn't overdo it, you know. I'll get in some nice cakes for your tea.

GEORGE: Please don't do that, Mrs Elliot dear, you know I don't eat them.

MRS ELLIOT: All right, dear, just as you like. [*Going to him.*] I'm ever so sorry about the money, dear. Something will turn up soon I expect – don't worry, dear. Raymond's money didn't go as far as we thought it might, did it? Still, never mind. As long as I've got a shilling or two, I'll see that you're all right. Now I really must go and get some shopping done. I hate Saturdays – the crowds are awful. [*Crosses into hall, and puts on coat.*]

[*The doorbell rings.*]

Oh, that'll be the milkman. Now where's my bag? [*She picks it up from the hallstand, and goes to the front door.*] Oh yes, yes, he does. Won't you come in?

[MRS ELLIOT *stands back to admit a tall, official-looking man. He carries a brief-case.*]

MAN: Thank you.

[*They go through the hall towards the sitting room.*]

MRS ELLIOT: I'd better show you the way. He's not feeling so good today. Still, it'll be a nice break for him, having someone to chat to. [*In sitting room.*] George, dear, someone to see you. Well, I'll leave you to it, if you don't mind. [*Exit through front door.*]

MAN: You are Mr George Dillon?

GEORGE: That's right.

MAN: I'm from the National Assistance Board.

GEORGE: Oh yes, I wondered when you were coming. Please sit down.

MAN: Thank you.

[*He does so. Then opens brief-case, and extracts papers, file, etc., and fountain-pen from jacket. He studies papers for a moment.*]

Hmm. Now, with regard to your claim for assistance – you are Mr George Dillon?

GEORGE: I thought we'd cleared that up just now.

MAN [*making notes*]: And you are residing at this address, paying rent of thirty shillings a week?

GEORGE: Right.

MAN: What does that entail the use of? A bedroom, and general run of the house, I take it?

GEORGE: Yes.

MAN: May I trouble you for your rent book?

GEORGE: Well, as a matter of fact, I haven't got one. Not right now, that is. I could get you one, if it's really necessary.

MAN: You understand we have to examine your rent book, Mr Dillon, in order to ascertain the correctness of your statement regarding the thirty shillings which you claim is being paid out by you in the way of rent each week.

GEORGE: Yes, of course.

MAN: So would you please make sure you are in possession of one, the next time I call.

GEORGE: Does that mean that I'll have to wait until then before I get any money?

[PERCY *comes in at the front door.*]

MAN: I'm afraid I can't answer that at the moment, Mr Dillon. Now, let me see. You are, by profession, an actor?

GEORGE: Yes, I am – by profession.

MAN: Have you any idea when you are likely to be working again?

GEORGE: It's rather difficult to say.

MAN: In the near future, would it be?

GEORGE: That phone might ring at this moment with something for me. Or it may not ring for months. It might not even ring at all.

MAN: You seem to have chosen a very precarious profession, Mr Dillon.

GEORGE: This money means rather a lot at the moment. I need – something – to show, you see –

MAN: Isn't there something else you could do, in the meantime perhaps?

GEORGE: Do you think I haven't tried? Incidentally, I am rather anxious that no one in the house should know about this –

MAN: Yes, of course.

[PERCY *enters sitting room, and sits down.*]

MAN: Yes. I see. Well, Mr Dillon, I can only hand in my report as I see things, and see what happens. The board is very hesitant about – paying out money to strong, healthy men.

GEORGE: Of course. Is there anything else? [*Looking at Percy. The* ASSISTANCE MAN *is not quite sure what to do.*]

MAN: There's just the little matter of your last job. When was that?

GEORGE: Oh, about three months ago – television.

PERCY: Accch! You don't call that a job, do you? You could hardly see it was him. *We* knew it was him all right – but you had to be sharp to catch him.

MAN: Well, that'll be all I think, Mr Dillon. [*Rising.*] You won't forget your rent book, will you?

PERCY: Rent book. Rent book! He hasn't got one! Shouldn't think he's ever paid any!

GEORGE: He knows that, you idiot. Well, I'll show you to the door, shall I?

[GEORGE *shows him into the hall. They get to the foot of the stairs, and the* MAN *turns.*]

MAN [*officialdom relaxing*]: You know, you people are a funny lot. I don't understand you. Look what you do to yourselves. And all for what? What do you get out of it? It beats me. Now take me and my wife. We don't have any worries. I've got my job during the day – secure, pension at the end of it. Mrs Webb is at home, looking after the kiddies – she knows there'll be a pay-packet every Friday. And in the evenings, we sit at home together, or sometimes we'll go out. But we're happy. There's quite a lot to it, you know. [*Quite kindly.*] What could be better? I ask you? No, you think it over, son. You think it over.

[*He goes out of the front door.* JOSIE *comes downstairs in her dressing-gown.*]

JOSIE [*quietly*]: Ruth home yet?

GEORGE: No. Not yet.

JOSIE: Know where she is?

GEORGE: She's at the doctor's.

JOSIE: Doctor's? What for?

GEORGE: For me. [*Crossing to sitting room.*]

JOSIE: For you? Thought you didn't believe in doctors.

GEORGE [*turns*]: I don't. She's picking something up for me.

JOSIE [*going to him*]: I should have thought you could have done that rather well yourself. What's she picking up for you?

GEORGE: What's called a report. You know? Making no progress, but he mustn't try so hard. Unpromising.

JOSIE: Oh, I see. [*Crossing through into kitchen.*] Think I'll have some hot milk.

[GEORGE *goes into the sitting room after her, and picks up the scattered leaves of his manuscript.*]

PERCY: Well, young man – you're at it again I see.

GEORGE: Yes, I'm afraid I'm not getting very far with it though.

PERCY: I don't mean that. I mean you're busy fleecing money from someone else again.

GEORGE: What the hell are you talking about?

PERCY: Not content with taking the money we bring home, you're even trying to get hold of the money we pay in income tax. You're getting it all ways, aren't you, George?

GEORGE: I certainly am! Look here, Percy, you'd better be careful what you say –

PERCY: And I think you'd better be careful what *you* say. Telling a government official barefaced lies like that! That's a case – [*leaning forward with infinite relish*] – for the assizes, that is!

GEORGE: All right, I admit it. But Mrs Elliot knows that she'll get back every penny, and more, for looking after me as she has.

PERCY: Accch! I don't believe it. Anyway, you don't think she'll be very pleased when she finds out where it comes from, do you? Assistance Board! To think of us having someone like that at the door. What'll people think of that? I know all about you my lad. I've checked up on you at my firm – you owe bills all over the place. Don't be surprised if you don't have the police after you soon – for debt. *Debt!* [*Thrilling with horror*] Imagine that! Police coming to my house – to me that's never owed a farthing to anybody in all his life.

[*Doorbell rings, followed by violent knocking.*]

PERCY: And it wouldn't surprise me if that was them already. I know a copper's knock when I hear it.

[*Exit quickly into kitchen.* GEORGE *sinks into arm-chair, exhausted. Doorbell and knocking again. Pause.* BARNEY EVANS *comes in through the front door. He is wearing a rather old Crombie overcoat, an expensive but crumpled suit, thick horn-rimmed glasses, and a rakish brown Homburg hat. He is nearly fifty, and has never had a doubt about anything in all that time.*]

BARNEY: Anyone there? Anyone at home? I say?

GEORGE: In here. Come in here.

BARNEY: Where? [*To sitting room.*] In here? Oh yes. Good. Sorry to butt in on you like this. The fact is – [GEORGE *rises.*] Oh yes, you must be who I am looking for.

GEORGE: Oh? Sit down, will you?

BARNEY: No, no, no – I can't stop a minute. I found I was passing your door, so I thought I'd just pop in for a few words. I haven't a London office any longer – just for a moment, you see. I'm just on my way to Brighton, as a matter of fact.

GEORGE: For the week-end?

BARNEY: Business and pleasure. [*Thoughtfully.*] Business – mostly. Look, I'll come straight to the point, Mr –

GEORGE: Dillon. George Dillon.

BARNEY [*producing a script from his pocket*]: Oh yes. It's on here. George Dillon. Been in the business long?

GEORGE: Well – a few –

BARNEY: Thought so. Didn't ever play the Palace, Westport, did you?

GEORGE: No, I didn't.

BARNEY: Face seemed familiar. Well, now – to get down to it –

GEORGE: Is that my script you've got there?

BARNEY: That's right.

GEORGE: How on earth did you get hold of it?

BARNEY: Andy gave it to me.

GEORGE: Andy?

BARNEY: André Tetlock. You know him, don't you?

GEORGE: Oh — the Trident. Is he a friend of yours then?

BARNEY: Andy? I knew him when he was a chorus boy at the old Tivoli. You wouldn't remember that. Why, it was me put him back on his feet after that bit of trouble. You know that don't you?

GEORGE: Yes?

BARNEY: He hadn't even got a set of underwear — I had to get that for him. Silly fellow! [*Sucks in his breath deprecatingly.*] Still, he's all right now. That was my idea — that bar, you know. Oh, he did it up himself, mind you — Andy's very clever with his hands. But it was my idea. And now that bar's packed every night. Can't get within a mile of the place. He doesn't have to worry whether he puts on a show or not. Get some odd types there, of course, but you know Andy — so everybody's happy. And as long as he can find enough authors willing to back their own plays with hard cash, *he* won't go without his bottle of gin, believe me. [*Produces a packet of cheroots.*] Got a match? I take it you *don't* have any capital of your own?

GEORGE: Right.

BARNEY: Yes, he said you'd told him you hadn't any money to put up yourself.

GEORGE [*lighting his cheroot for him*]: I rang him about it weeks ago. I remember he said he'd liked the play, but he'd passed it on to someone else.

BARNEY: Liked it! That's a good one. Andy doesn't *read* plays — he just puts 'em on. Provided of course he can make something out of it! Now, I've read this play of yours, and I'm interested. Are you willing to listen to a proposition?

GEORGE: Of course.

BARNEY: By the way, I'm Barney Evans. You've heard of me, of course?

   [GEORGE *hesitates, but* BARNEY *doesn't wait.*]

Now, Andy's a friend of mine. I've done a lot for him — but he's only in the business in a very small way. Oh, he does himself all right. But it's small stuff. You wouldn't get anywhere much with him – You know that, of course?

GEORGE: Yes.

BARNEY: I'm only interested in the big money. Small stuff's not worth my while. I take it you *are* interested in money?

GEORGE: Is that a rhetorical question?

BARNEY: Eh?

GEORGE: Yes, I am.

BARNEY: That's all right then. I don't want to waste my time. This the first play you've written?

GEORGE: My seventh –

BARNEY: Dialogue's not bad, but these great long speeches – that's a mistake. People want action, excitement. I know – *you* think you're Bernard Shaw. But where's he today? Eh? People won't listen to him. Anyway, politics are out – you ought to know that. Now, take *My Skin is my Enemy!* I've got that on the road at the moment. That and *Slasher Girl!*

GEORGE: *My Skin is my* – Oh yes, it's about the colour bar problem, isn't it?

BARNEY: Well, yes – but you see it's first-class entertainment! Played to £600 at Llandrindod Wells last week. Got the returns in my pocket now. It's controversial, I grant you, but it's the kind of thing people pay money to see. That's the kind of thing you want to write.

GEORGE: Still, I imagine you've got to be just a bit liberal-minded to back a play like that.

BARNEY: Eh?

GEORGE: I mean – putting on a play about coloured people.

BARNEY: Coloured people? I hate the bastards! You should talk to the author about them. He can't even be civil to them. No – I know young fellows like you. You're interested in ideals still. Idealists. Don't think I don't know. I was an idealist myself once. I could tell you a lot, only I haven't got time now. But, make no mistake – ideals didn't get me where I am.

GEORGE: No?

BARNEY: You spend your time dabbling in politics, and vote in some ragged-arsed bunch of nobodies, who can't hardly pronounce the Queen's English properly, and where are you? Where are you? Nowhere. Crushed down in the mob, indistinguishable from the masses. What's the good of that to a young man with talent?

GEORGE: I should have thought you had a vested interest in the masses.

BARNEY: Most certainly. I admit it. And that's why I believe in education. Education — it always shows, and it always counts. That's why I say let them who've got it run the whole show. We're not going to get anywhere with these foreigners once they see they're no longer dealing with gentlemen. They're always impressed by an English gentleman. Just because they've got no breeding themselves, they know how to recognize it in others when they see it. Oh, yes. I could tell you a lot you don't know. However, I am diverting from what I came about.

[*He sprays his ash over the floor thoughtfully.*]

To get back to this play of yours. I think it's got possibilities, but it needs rewriting. Acts One and Two won't be so bad, provided you cut out all the highbrow stuff, give it pace — you know: dirty it up a bit, you see.

GEORGE: I see.

BARNEY: Third Act's construction is weak. I could help you there — and I'd do it for quite a small consideration because I think you've got something. You know that's a very good idea — getting the girl in the family way.

GEORGE: You think so?

BARNEY: Never fails. Get someone in the family way in the Third Act — you're halfway there. I suppose you saw *I Was a Drug Fiend*?

GEORGE: No.

BARNEY: Didn't you really? No wonder you write like you do! I thought everyone had seen that! That was my show too. Why, we were playing to three and four thousand a week on the twice-nightly circuit with that. That's the sort of money you want to play to. Same thing in that: Third Act – girl's in the family way. Course, in that play, her elder sister goes out as a missionary and ends up dying upside down on an ant hill in her birthday suit. I spent six months in the South of France on what I made out of that show. [*Motor-horn toots outside.*] Here, I'll have to be going. As I say, you rewrite it as I tell you, maybe we can do business together and make some money for both of us. I'll read it through again, and drop you a line. In the meantime, I should redraft the whole thing, bearing in mind what I said. Right.

GEORGE: I'll have to think about it. The fact is – I'm not feeling up to much at the moment. I'm completely broke for one thing.

BARNEY: O.K. then. You'll be hearing from me. You take my advice – string along with me. I know this business inside and out. You forget about starving for Art's sake. That won't keep you alive five minutes. You've got to be ruthless. [*Moves into hall.*] Yes, there's no other word for it – absolutely ruthless. [GEORGE *follows him.*]

[BARNEY *picks up his hat from stand and knocks over the vase. He looks down at the pieces absent-mindedly.*]

BARNEY: Oh, sorry. Now you take Hitler – the greatest man that ever lived! Don't care what anyone says – you can't get away from it. He had the right idea, you've got to be ruthless, and it's the same in this business. Course he may have gone a bit too far sometimes.

GEORGE: Think so?

BARNEY: I do. I do think so, most definitely. Yes, he over-reached himself, no getting away from it. That's where all great men make their mistake – they over-reach themselves.

[*The car horn toots more insistently.*]

Hullo, blimey, she'll start smashing the windows in a minute. [GEORGE *follows him as he hurries to door.*] Well, you just remember what I said. Tell you what – I'll give you a ring on Monday. I'll be busy all the week-end. [*Opens door.*] By the way, that girl?

GEORGE: What girl?

BARNEY: The girl in your play – what do you call her?

GEORGE: Oh, you mean –

BARNEY: Build her up. Build her right up. She's – she's a prostitute *really* isn't she?

GEORGE: Well –

BARNEY: Of course she is! I've just had an idea – a new slant. Your title, what is it? [*He doesn't wait for a reply.*] Anyway, it won't bring anybody in. I've just thought of a smashing title. You know what we'll call it? *Telephone Tart*, that's it! *Telephone Tart*. You string along with me, George, I'll see you're all right. [*Exit.*]

[JOSIE *looks in from kitchen.*]

JOSIE [*coming in, with a glass of milk*]: It's all right, he's gone. [*Sits in arm-chair.*] Don't know what all the fuss was about.

PERCY: Well, I hadn't shaved, you see. I should hate to let George down in front of his friends – what few he *has* got.

JOSIE: Oh, you are daft, Dad. You don't know what you're talking about half the time.

[GEORGE *comes slowly into sitting room.*]

JOSIE: Who was it, George? Teddy-bear coat and all!

GEORGE [*smiling wryly*]: I suppose he's what you might call the poor man's Binkie.

JOSIE: What? Whatever's that? What's that, George?

[RUTH *comes in front door into sitting room.*]

GEORGE: Oh, never mind. It doesn't really matter. Hello, Ruth.

RUTH [*after a slight pause*]: Hullo.

GEORGE: Well, did you go to the doctor's?

RUTH: Yes.

GEORGE: Well – [*laughing*] – don't stand there with the angel of death on your shoulder – what did he say?

RUTH: George – just come in here, will you, for a minute.

[GEORGE *follows her into lounge.*]

JOSIE: Well, of all the – I like that, I must say! We're not good enough to know what's going on! [*Rising and going up to radiogram.*] I'm sure I don't want to hear what she got to say to George. Them and their secrets. [*She puts on Mambo record very loud.*]

[*JOSIE then picks up a magazine and glances at it viciously, her foot wagging furiously. After a moment she gets up and goes over to the window and looks out in the same manner. PERCY watches her all the time. She catches him doing it.*]

JOSIE: Well, had your eyeful?

[*She walks over-casually towards the lounge door.*]

Real heart-to-heart they're having, aren't they?

[*Over to mirror as RUTH comes out of the lounge and goes into the sitting room and says something to PERCY. MRS ELLIOT comes in at the front door, laden as usual. She goes into sitting room and switches off the radiogram.*]

MRS ELLIOT: Whatever do you want that thing on like that for, Josie? I could hear it halfway down the street. I thought you weren't well?

[*Pause.*]

Why, what is it? What's the matter with you all? What is it, Ruth?

PERCY [*in a voice like sandpaper*]: George has got T.B.

MRS ELLIOT: T.B., George. I don't believe it. It isn't true. There must be some mistake –

RUTH: There's no mistake. It's quite true, Kate. The doctor will be coming up soon to let us know what the arrangements are.

MRS ELLIOT: Does this mean that he'll have to go away?

[*RUTH nods her head.*]

George – poor old George. [*She moves into hall and up the stairs.*] George dear, where are you? He won't like this at all, will he? George –

[*PERCY comes out of room to foot of stairs as MRS ELLIOT is half-way up.*]

PERCY [*calling up loudly*]: You'll have to burn everything, you know! All his sheets, blankets. Everything will have to be burnt, you know!

JOSIE: Oh, my God. Auntie Ruth! What's going to happen. What about me?

RUTH: You?

JOSIE: Yes, that's what I want to know – what's going to happen to me?

QUICK CURTAIN

SCENE 2

Winter.

[MRS ELLIOT *is on stage alone. She is looking up the stairs. George's hat, coat, and suitcase are standing in the hall. She is looking very anxious. She picks up the hat and coat, and hangs them up carefully on the hall-stand. Then she goes back to the sitting room. She goes over to the wedding group picture, and stares up at it. As she is doing this* PERCY *comes in at the front door. He takes off his hat and coat, hangs them up beside George's, and comes into the sitting room.*]

PERCY: So he's back then?

MRS ELLIOT: Yes.

PERCY: Where is he?

MRS ELLIOT: Upstairs – talking to Josie.

PERCY: Upstairs?

MRS ELLIOT: Yes. She wasn't feeling too good this morning, so I told her to stay in bed. I didn't want to take any chances. I think she was over-excited at the thought of George coming back.

PERCY: Excited, was she?

MRS ELLIOT: Of course she was. She's thought about nothing else for weeks.

PERCY: Well, well! She's in for a bit of a shock, isn't she?

MRS ELLIOT: Listen to me, Percy. I've told you – you're to keep out of this. It's nothing to do with you. The only two people it need concern at the moment are George and myself. Above all, I don't want one word of this to get to Josie's ears. We've no idea what might happen if she was to get a shock like that. And in her present condition. If you so much as open your mouth about it to her – you can pack your bags and go. You understand? Besides, we don't know yet that it's true – not for certain. We've only got your word for it, and we all know what a nasty mind you've got. It would please you to think something rotten of George. You've always been against him. You're jealous of him – that's why.

PERCY: Me? Jealous of him! That wreck!

MRS ELLIOT: He's a gentleman – which is something you'll never be.

PERCY: Oh, he is, is he? Perhaps that's why he can't even earn the price of a cup of tea!

MRS ELLIOT: That's all *you* know.

PERCY: And what does that mean, exactly?

MRS ELLIOT: Never you mind. But there's a lot you don't know about George. George will come out tops in the end – you wait.

PERCY: Seems more like there was a lot *all* of us didn't know about him.

MRS ELLIOT: You don't understand, Percy. And what's more, you never will. You think everyone's like yourself. George is an artist –

PERCY: And what's *that* supposed to mean?

MRS ELLIOT: He's sensitive, proud – he suffers deeply. Raymond was like that – you never liked him, and he was your own son. That boy's gone through a lot – he doesn't have to tell me that. I could tell the first time I ever spoke to him. I knew he was a good fellow, that all he wanted was a chance to bring a little pleasure to other people. I don't think that's so much of a crime, anyway. Oh, he's never said anything to me, but I've known what he's been going through all these months. When he's come back here in the evenings, when he couldn't get a job or any kind of encouragement at all, when people like you were sneering at him, and nobody wanted him. He didn't think I knew when he was feeling sick with disappointment. He didn't think I knew he was trying to pass it off by making us laugh, and pretending that everything was going to be all right. And I've never been able to tell him because I can't express myself properly – not like he can. He's got a gift for it – that's why he's an artist. That's why he's different from us. But he'll have his own way in the end, you mark my words. He'll show them all – and you. God always pays debts without money. I've got down on my knees at night, and prayed for that boy. I've prayed that he'll be well, and get on, and be happy – here – with us.

PERCY: With us?

MRS ELLIOT: If that's what he wants. And I believe it is. I know we're not the kind of people George is used to, and probably likes being with – he must have felt it sometimes. Not that he's ever said anything – he's too well brought up for that. He just accepts us for what we are. He's settled in here. And while he's been in that hospital all these weeks, he's known he's got somewhere to come back to. He's known that somebody wants him, anyway, and that's a great deal when you're laying there in bed, and you don't know properly whether you're going to live or die. To know that some-one is counting the days until you come home.

PERCY: What's he look like?

MRS ELLIOT: A bit thin. But who wouldn't look thin on that hospital food? I'll soon feed him up.

PERCY: Did you manage to have a word with the doctor?

MRS ELLIOT: No, I didn't.

PERCY: Well, why not?

MRS ELLIOT: Because I wasn't going to ask the doctor a lot of questions behind George's back, that's why. He's back – that's all I care about, that's all I want to know at the moment. Things will work themselves out somehow. George won't let us down.

PERCY: Well, we shall soon see, shan't we? He's a long time up there, don't you think? And what's he going to do about his wife?

MRS ELLIOT: How do I know what he's going to do? Why can't

you shut up about it! You've talked about nothing else for days now.

PERCY: You mean to say you didn't tackle him about it?

MRS ELLIOT: I didn't have an opportunity. I couldn't bring it up on the bus, could I? Besides, I couldn't start on him straight away. And as soon as we got back, he wanted to go up and see Josie, naturally.

PERCY: Well, you wait till he comes down. If you're afraid to tackle him about it, I'm not.

MRS ELLIOT: I meant what I said, you know. If you try and cause trouble in this house, you can go.

PERCY: I think it's disgusting. Carrying on in someone else's house – a married man at that! Do you know what? It's my belief that there was something between him and your sister Ruth – and that's why she decided to pack her bags, and go, all of a sudden.

MRS ELLIOT: Oh, don't be so childish, for heaven's sake, Percy. You've got sex on the brain. I must admit you could have knocked me down when Ruth told me she was going to find herself a room somewhere. I mean – it seemed a bit suspicious. She didn't even give a proper explanation. Just said that she felt she had to 'get out of it'. It seemed a funny thing to say, and especially after all these years. Of course, she always was a dark horse. But, as for her and George – it's ridiculous. Why, she's old enough to be his mother.

PERCY [*as he goes to lounge*]: Oh, you women – you go on and on.

[RUTH *appears at front door – unlocking it, enters, leaving door open.* RUTH *enters sitting room.*]

RUTH [*quietly*]: Kate. Kate.

[GEORGE *comes downstairs – shuts front door. Then goes towards sitting room – meets* RUTH *face to face in the doorway.*)

RUTH: Hello, George. Are you better?

GEORGE: You're not really going, are you?

RUTH: I was coming to collect my things this morning – but I couldn't.

GEORGE: In fact it's quite a coincidence meeting you.

RUTH: No. Not really. I suppose it was silly of me to come when I knew you'd be back. I always seem to let myself in for farewells.

GEORGE: We both ought to be pretty good at them by now. [*Pause.*] Are you really leaving then?

RUTH: Not again, please. There's only a few minutes.

GEORGE [*very quietly*]: What's going to happen to me?

RUTH: George – don't! Try and help a little.

[*Pause.*]

GEORGE: Isn't it hell – loving people?

RUTH: Yes – hell.

GEORGE: Still sounds rather feeble when you say it though. Rather like 'shift me – I'm burning'. What are you going to do?

RUTH: I don't know. Maybe find some scruffy wretch with a thumb-nail sketch of a talent, and spend my time emptying bits of brown cigarette stubs from his saucer – generally cleaning up.

GEORGE: Did you ever look up your – friend?

[*He lifts up the wrist-watch.*]

RUTH: Yes. I did. Soon after you came in here. But he wasn't at the same place any more. His landlord gave me his new address. Number something Eaton Square.

GEORGE: But of course, my dear – everyone lives in Eaton Square.

RUTH: Apparently, she's in publishing. She's just published his book last week. But I mustn't be unfair – she didn't write the reviews as well. They fairly raved. He's on top of the world.

GEORGE: You know I've been waiting for you to tell me that you're old enough to be my mother. Still, mothers don't walk out on their sons – or do they?

RUTH: How's Josie – have you seen her yet?

GEORGE: God! What a farce! What pure, screaming farce!

[*He starts to laugh.*]

RUTH: For heaven's sake!

GEORGE: Sorry. I just thought of something. How to make sure of your Third Act. Never fails! [*Roars with laughter.*] Never fails!

[*Subsides almost immediately.*] Don't panic. I'll not get maudlin. I probably would start howling any minute, only I'm afraid of getting the bird from my best audience.

[*He looks away from her, and adds in a strangled voice, barely audible.*] Don't leave me on my own!

[*But he turns back quickly.*]

You haven't mentioned my – success – once.

RUTH: I didn't know whether you expected me to congratulate you or not.

GEORGE: Second week of tour – I've got the returns here. Look: Empire Theatre, Llandrindod Wells – week's gross takings £647 18s. 4d. Long-hair drama gets a haircut from Mr Barney Evans!

RUTH: I simply can't bear to go on watching you any longer.

GEORGE: But don't you think it's all very comic? I seem to remember some famous comedian saying once that he'd never seen anything funny that wasn't terrible. So don't think I'll mind if you laugh. I expect it. We should be both good for a titter, anyway. That's why religion is so damned deadly – it's not even good for a giggle. And what's life without a good giggle, eh? That's what I always say! Isn't that what you always say, Ruth?

RUTH: Let go of my hand. You're hurting me.

GEORGE: Well – isn't it? No. Perhaps it isn't. We never really had the same sense of humour, after all.

RUTH: Please don't try to hurt yourself any more by trying to hit back at me. I know how you feel. You're overcome with failure. Eternal bloody failure.

GEORGE: But I'm not a failure, I'm a – success.

RUTH: Are you, George? [*She turns away.*]

GEORGE: Listen! I'll make you laugh yet, before you go. Just a trip on the stage-cloth, and Lear teeters on, his crown round his ears, his grubby tights full of moth-holes. How they all long for those tights to fall down. What a relief it would be! Oh, we should all use stronger elastic. And the less sure we are of our pathetic little

divine rights, the stronger the elastic we should use. You've seen
the whole, shabby, solemn pretence now. That is where you came
in. For God's sake go.

[*She turns to go.*]

GEORGE: No, wait. Shall I recite my epitaph to you? Yes, do recite
your epitaph to me. 'Here lies the body of George Dillon, aged
thirty-four – or thereabouts – who thought, who hoped, he was
that mysterious, ridiculous being called an artist. He never allowed
himself one day of peace. He worshipped the physical things of
this world, and was betrayed by his own body. He loved also the
things of the mind, but his own brain was a cripple from the waist
down. He achieved nothing he set out to do. He made no one
happy, no one looked up with excitement when he entered the room.
He was always troubled with wind round his heart, but he loved
no one successfully. He was a bit of a bore, and, frankly, rather
useless. But the germs loved him. [*He doesn't see* RUTH *as she goes
out and up the stairs.*] Even his sentimental epitaph is probably a
pastiche of someone or other, but he doesn't quite know who.
And, in the end, it doesn't really matter.' [*He turns, but* RUTH *has
gone.*]

[*Bell rings,* PERCY *opens door.*]

NORAH [*coming in*]: Only me. Forgot my key again. Is George back
yet? [*Into room.*] George! You are back!

GEORGE: Yes, Norah, I'm back again, with a face like the death of
kings.

NORAH [*rushes to him*]: Oh, George, you look fine! Doesn't he, Dad?
I thought you'd look awful – but you look fine. [*Kisses him as*
MRS ELLIOT *comes in from kitchen.*]

GEORGE: Here – mind my ribs!

NORAH: Oh, we'll soon feed you up, won't we, Mum?

[*She takes him into sitting room,* PERCY *follows.*]

MRS ELLIOT: We certainly will. We're going to look after him from
now on. He can sit in here all day and rest, and – keep himself
happy. Can't you, George?

GEORGE: Rather.

MRS ELLIOT: He can lie down on the settee in the afternoons with his books and things, and – oh, I forgot! We got you a little home-coming present, didn't we, Norah?

NORAH: Shall I go up and get it?

MRS ELLIOT: If you like, dear, I don't know whether George feels up to opening presents. He must feel all in after that journey. I expect he'd like a bit of a rest.

GEORGE: I'm all right. I'd like a cup of tea though.

MRS ELLIOT: It's all ready. And I'll get you something to eat in no time.

NORAH: All right, then. I'll go and get it. I'll just pop in and have a look at Josie. Have you seen her, George?

MRS ELLIOT: He's been in there ever since he came in, haven't you, George?

NORAH [*crossing to and up stairs*]: She's been so excited at the thought of you coming back. She's talked about nothing else for days. [*She laughs.*] Isn't love grand!
   [*Exit.*]

MRS ELLIOT: It's true, George. She's been quite a changed girl since you went away. I'm afraid she did used to be a bit on the lazy side sometimes, but not now – you wouldn't know her. Why, Sunday we spent practically all evening getting your room ready and looking nice. And Norah's been the same. Why, she's even booked seats for a coach ride for all of us down to the seaside.

PERCY: Well? How are you feeling, George?

GEORGE: Sorry, Percy. I haven't had a chance to say hullo yet, have I? [*Offers his hand.*]

PERCY [*shakes perfunctorily*]: How have they been treating you?

GEORGE: Oh, not too bad, thanks. But it's certainly good to be back. You've all given me such a welcome.

PERCY: It's quite a nice place down there, I believe.

GEORGE: It's all right.

PERCY: Nice country.

GEORGE: Oh, lovely.

PERCY: Isn't that near Tunbridge Wells?

GEORGE: Not far.

MRS ELLIOT: I don't suppose he wants to talk much now, Percy. Let him have a rest first. He's tired.

PERCY: They say that's a nice town.

GEORGE: It's pleasant enough.

PERCY: Ever been there, George?

GEORGE: What are you getting at?

PERCY: I think you *know* what I'm getting at.

GEORGE [*to Mrs Elliot*]: What is it? You're upset about something, aren't you. I could tell something was wrong when you met me at the hospital. And all the way home on the bus.

PERCY: I suppose you didn't happen to be in Tunbridge Wells on June 22nd, 1943, did you?

[*Pause.*]

GEORGE: I see.

MRS ELLIOT: George – it's not true, is it? I was sure he'd made a mistake.

GEORGE: No, he hasn't made a mistake. I *was* married in Tunbridge Wells, and it was in 1943. The middle of June. It poured with rain. How did you find out?

PERCY: Through my firm, as a matter of fact. As you know, it's our job to check on people's credentials, etc., for hire purchase firms and the like. Well, last week, I found myself checking on a certain Ann Scott, on behalf of a building society. She's contemplating buying some big property in Chelsea. Good report – excellent banker's references and all that. Living in large house in upper-class district. And it seems her married name is Mrs George Dillon. Well? What have you got to say?

GEORGE: Well?

MRS ELLIOT: Oh, dear.

GEORGE: What do you want me to say?

MRS ELLIOT: I don't know, George. I'm so upset, I don't know where I am. I suppose it's not your fault, but –

GEORGE: But, my dear, I don't see what there is to be so upset about. This doesn't change anything.

MRS ELLIOT: But – but what about Josie?

GEORGE: Nothing is changed, I tell you. It's simply that neither my wife nor I have ever bothered about a divorce. She's had other things to think about, and I've never had the money. But it's all easily settled. There's nothing to worry about. I promise you.

MRS ELLIOT: You're not just saying this, George? I'd rather –

GEORGE: Of course not. I've come home, haven't I?

MRS ELLIOT: Yes, you have. You've come home, thank heaven.

GEORGE: You see, my wife never was anything. With Josie, it's different. I know exactly where I am.

MRS ELLIOT: She loves you, George. She really does.

GEORGE: Yes. I know.

PERCY: It said on my report that she's an actress, this wife of yours.
[PERCY *feels cheated, and is desperately looking for something else.*]

GEORGE: Right.

PERCY: She must do pretty well at it then.

GEORGE: She does.

PERCY: Can't say I've ever heard the name.

GEORGE: On the contrary, you know her very well.

PERCY: What do you mean?

GEORGE: I mean that somebody must have slipped up rather badly in your report. They seem to have left out her stage name.

PERCY: Stage name?

GEORGE: We both thought 'Ann Scott' a bit commonplace.

PERCY: Who is she then?

GEORGE: Well, you've always told me that she's the only one in your favourite television parlour game who's really any good at all. In fact, you've said so many times.

PERCY: You don't mean – What? Not *her*!

GEORGE: Her.

PERCY: Well, I'll be . . .

GEORGE: Yes. It's always puzzled me why you should admire her so much. Or anyone else for that matter.

MRS ELLIOT: But George – honestly, I don't know where I am. Now that – well – now that you're a success, how do you know that your wife won't want you back?

GEORGE: Somehow, I don't think that will influence her!

PERCY: What are you talking about? Now that he's a success?

MRS ELLIOT [recovered and triumphant]: Well, I don't see why he shouldn't know now, do you, George?

GEORGE: No, I don't see why not.

MRS ELLIOT: George has had his play put on. It's on tour at the moment, and last week it made – tell him how much it made, George.

GEORGE: £647 18s. 4d. [Flourishing returns.]

MRS ELLIOT: And he gets five per cent of that every week, so perhaps that will shut you up a bit.

PERCY [staring at returns]: Well! Fancy that! Why didn't somebody tell me?

MRS ELLIOT: Why should they? Well, I mustn't stand here wasting time. You must be hungry, George.

[Phone rings.]

MRS ELLIOT: Do answer that, Percy, will you? Wish Norah would hurry up.

[PERCY goes to phone. NORAH comes down stairs carrying parcel into sitting room.]

NORAH: Josie says she won't be long, she's going to get up.

PERCY: What's that? Oh, yes, hang on a minute while I find my pencil. All right – go ahead.

NORAH: Well, George, here we are – I can't wait to see his face when he opens it, Mum.

GEORGE: Well –

MRS ELLIOT: No, wait till Josie comes down. She'll want to be with him when he opens it.

NORAH: Oh, blow that. She's got all the time in the world with him now. If he won't open it, I will.

PERCY: Yes. Yes. I've got that. Who? What? What name? Right. Good-bye.

MRS ELLIOT: All right then. I don't suppose she'll mind. Go on, George, open it.

[GEORGE *starts opening the parcel.*]

PERCY [*coming in*]: That was for you, George. A telegram.

GEORGE: Oh, who from?

PERCY: Somebody called Barney. I've got it written down here.

GEORGE: Read it out, will you? I'm busy at the moment.

PERCY: It says 'Playing capacity business. May this be the first of many smash hits together. Welcome home – Barney'.

MRS ELLIOT: Well, wasn't that nice of him?

GEORGE: Yes, good old Barney. Now, what have we here?

[*Stands back to reveal a portable typewriter.*]

Well! Look at that!

MRS ELLIOT: I hope you like it, George.

GEORGE: Like it! I should think I do! I think it must be the nicest present I've had. What can I say? [*He kisses them both.*] Thank you both. Thank you for everything.

MRS ELLIOT: That's all right, George. Believe me, all my prayers have been answered. Mr Colwyn-Stuart prayed for you too, every week you were away. All I want is for us all to be happy. Come along now, sit down, while I get the supper. Give him a chair, Percy, you look all in, dear.

PERCY: Oh, sorry. Here you are.

NORAH: It'll be nice, having George for a brother-in-law.

GEORGE: Yes, of course it will, Norah. It's about time you got married yourself, isn't it?

MRS ELLIOT: She almost has been –

NORAH: – Twice.

GEORGE: I'm sorry.

MRS ELLIOT: The last one was an American.

NORAH: Yes. The last time I saw him, we were going to get a bus to Richmond. He just simply said suddenly: 'Well, so long, honey, it's been nice knowing you' and got on a bus going in the opposite direction. It's swimming on the telly tonight. I think I'll go and watch it, if you'll excuse me.

[*She goes into lounge. Slight pause.*]

MRS ELLIOT: Well, I don't know. What with one thing and another! That's right, George dear. Just you relax from now on. And you let him alone, Percy. I've always believed in you, George. Always. I knew he'd come out tops.

[MRS ELLIOT *goes into kitchen.* GEORGE *leans back, tired.* PERCY *turns on radio. Jazz* — '*If you can't give me a dollar give me a lousy dime.*']

PERCY: Not too loud for you, George?

GEORGE: No — fine. [*Pause.*]

PERCY: I can't get over it you know.

GEORGE: What?

PERCY: Your wife, I mean. Big star like that. Surprised she couldn't have helped you on a bit all this time. Still, you're doing all right yourself now, by the look of it. Turned out to be Bernard Shaw, after all, eh? I suppose you'll be writing some more plays when you start feeling better again?

GEORGE: I dare say.

PERCY: I see. Same sort of thing?

[RUTH *comes down slowly with suitcase.*]

GEORGE: Yes. Same sort of thing.

PERCY: Well, that's good, isn't it? What was the name of that theatre again?

GEORGE: The Empire Theatre, Llandrindod Wells.

[*The sound of* JOSIE'S *voice singing comes from upstairs. From the lounge, the telly is playing music.*]

PERCY: Well, I don't think it would do any harm if we all have a little drink on this. [*To cocktail cabinet.*] If we're going to start living in style, we may as well get into the way of using this, eh?

[*He opens the cocktail cabinet, revealing all its hidden glory.* RUTH *exits through front door.*]

PERCY: Now, where are we. [*Staring into cabinet.*]

MRS ELLIOT: That's right. Let's have a little drink.

GEORGE [*in a flat, empty voice*]: Yes, let's have a little drink – to celebrate.

PERCY: Music, too, would not be inappropriate. [*Putting on record.*]

GEORGE: Music, too, would not be inappropriate.

[JOSIE *sings, off.*]

PERCY: Well, we can't leave the blushing bride upstairs all on her own, can we? I'll give her a yell, shall I, George?

[*He goes out, calling upstairs.* GEORGE *goes to the door. He looks trapped and looks around the room and the objects in it; he notices the birds on the wall.*]

GEORGE: Those bloody birds!

[*Enter* MRS ELLIOT. *He stares at her as if for the first time, then his face breaks into a mechanical smile.*]

Come on, Mum, let's dance!

[*They dance together for a few moments.*]

SLOW CURTAIN

ARNOLD WESKER

The Kitchen

THE KITCHEN

First presented by The English Stage Society at The Royal Court
Theatre, London, on 13 September 1959, with the following cast:

MAGI	Alan Howard
FIRST WAITRESS	Jennifer Wallace
MAX	Tenniel Evans
MANGOLIS	Peter Gill
PAUL	Alfred Lynch
RAYMOND	James Culliford
ANNE	Patsy Byrne
SECOND WAITRESS	Tarn Bassett
THIRD WAITRESS	Mary Miller
FOURTH WAITRESS	Jeanne Watts
DIMITRI	Charles Kay
HANS	Christopher Sandford
ALFREDO	Jack Rodney
GASTON	David Ryder
MICHAEL	James Bolam
BERTHA	Gwen Nelson
NICHOLAS	Anthony Carrick
KEVIN	John Briggs
PETER	Robert Stephens
FRANK, SECOND CHEF	Kenneth Adams
FIRST CHEF	Arnold Yarrow
FIFTH WAITRESS	Ida Goldapple
SIXTH WAITRESS	Brenda Peters
SEVENTH WAITRESS	Sandra Miller
EIGHTH WAITRESS	Ann King
MR MARANGO	Nigel Davenport
MONIQUE	Anne Bishop
HEAD WAITER	Cecil Brock
TRAMP	Patrick O'Connell

Directed by John Dexter

The action of the play takes place in the kitchen of the Tivoli Restaurant

INTRODUCTION AND NOTES FOR THE
PRODUCER

THE lengthy explanations I am forced to make may be annoying; I am sorry, but they are necessary.

This is a play about a large kitchen in a restaurant called the Tivoli. All kitchens, especially during service, go insane. There is the rush, there are the petty quarrels, grumbles, false prides, and snobbery. Kitchen staff instinctively hate dining-room staff, and all of them hate the customer. He is the personal enemy. The world might have been a stage for Shakespeare, but to me it is a kitchen: where people come and go and cannot stay long enough to understand each other, and friendships, loves, and enmities are forgotten as quickly as they are made.

The quality of the food here is not so important as the speed with which it is served. Each person has his own particular job. We glance in upon him, high-lighting as it were the individual. But though we may watch just one or a group of people, the rest of the kitchen staff does not. They work on.

So, because activity must continue while the main action is played out, we shall study, together with a diagram of the kitchen, who comes in and what they do.

The waitresses spend the morning working in the dining room before they eat their lunch. But throughout the morning there are about three or four who wander in and out carrying glasses from the glasserie to the dining room. Others wander into the steam room emptying their buckets of water; they carry mops and they have scarves on their heads. One or two others perform duties which are mentioned in the course of the play. During the service, the waitresses are continually coming out of the dining room and ordering dishes from the cooks. The dishes are served on silver, and the waitresses take about six plates out of the hot-plate immediately under the serving-counter. Stocks of plates are replenished all the time by the porters. These are highly efficient waitresses. They make a circuit round the kitchen calling at the stations they require. They move fast and carry large quantities of dishes in their arms.

The kitchen porters, who are mixed Cypriots and Maltese, are divided into various sections. Firstly, there are those who do the actual washing of cutlery, tins, and plates by machine; these we do not see. But we do see the two porters by the swill. During the service the waitresses bring their dirty plates to the swill and these two porters push the remains of food into two holes leading to bins under the counter and push the dirty plates (out of sight) to the men at the machine. Two other porters continually replace clean plates under the serving-counter so that the waitresses can take them as required. Another sweeps up at regular intervals and throws sawdust around.

The woman who serves the cheeses and desserts we hardly and rarely see through the glass partition back of stage, but every now and then she comes to the pastry section to replenish her supplies of tarts and pastries. The coffee woman simply supplies cups of coffee from an urn to the waitresses as they call for it.

Now to the cooks. At this point it must be understood that at no time is food ever used. To cook and serve food is of course just not practical. Therefore the waitresses will carry empty dishes and the cooks will mime their cooking. Cooks being the main characters in this play, I shall sketch them and their activity here, so that while the main action of the play is continuing they shall always have something to do.

CHARACTERS OF THE PLAY
IN ORDER OF STATIONS

FRANK, *Second Chef, Poultry:* A prisoner of war for four years. Now at thirty-eight he has an easygoing nature. Nothing really upsets him, but then nothing excites him either. He drinks steadily throughout the day and by nightfall is blissfully drunk though instinctively capable. Flirts with the waitresses, squeezing their breasts and pinching their bottoms.

ALFREDO, *Roast:* An old chef, about sixty-five and flat-footed. Large-muscled and strong, though of medium height. He is a typical cook in that he will help nobody and will accept no help; nor will he impart his knowledge. He is the fastest worker there and sets-to straight away, not stopping till his station is all ready. He speaks little but has a dry sense of humour. He is the worker and the boss is the boss, and he probably despises the boss. He hums to himself as he works.

HANS, *Fry:* A German boy, nineteen, pimply, and adolescent. He is working in London through a system of exchange. He speaks very bad English and is impressed by anything flashy. Yet as a German he is sensitive.

PETER, *Boiled Fish:* Peter is the main character. Another young German aged twenty-three, who has worked at the Tivoli for the last three years. His parents were killed in the war. He is boisterous, aggressive, too merry, and yet good-natured. After three years at the Tivoli one might say he was living on his nerves. He speaks good English but with an accent, and when he is talking to people he tends to speak into their ear as though he were telling them a secret. It is a nervous movement. A strong characteristic of Peter is his laugh. It is a forced laugh, pronounced 'Hya Hya Hya' instead of 'Ha Ha Ha'. He turns this laugh into one of surprise or mockery, derision or simple merriment. There is also a song he sings (music on p. 98) which ends in exactly the same laughter. Somehow its maniacal tone is part of the whole atmosphere of the kitchen.

KEVIN, *Fried Fish:* The new young man, Irish, twenty-two. He spends most of his time being disturbed by the mad rush of the work and people around him. This is worse than anything he has ever seen.

GASTON, *Grill:* A Cypriot by birth, forty-odd, slight, and dark-complexioned. Everyone-is-his-friend until he starts work, and then he is inclined to go to pieces and panic and cry at everyone. When this play starts he has a loud scratch down the side of his face.

MICHAEL, *Eggs:* There is nothing particular about this boy of eighteen. He is what his dialogue will make him; but he is a cook and before long all cooks are infused with a kind of madness.

MAX, *Butcher:* A stout man of fifty. Loud-mouthed, smutty, and anti-anything that it is easy to be anti about. He has a cigarette continually drooping from his mouth and like Frank drinks steadily all day till he is drunk.

NICHOLAS, *Cold Buffet:* Nicholas is a young Cypriot who has lived in England three years and can therefore speak reasonable English but with an accent. Speaking the language and working in a capacity socially superior to his compatriots, who are dishwashers, he behaves with a wild heartiness, as one who is accepted. And as one who is accepted he imitates, and he chooses to imitate Frank and Max by becoming drunk by the end of the day.

RAYMOND AND PAUL, *Pastrycooks:* Paul is a young Jew; Raymond is an Italian who speaks almost perfect English but with an accent. These two pastrycooks, as opposed to the madmen in the kitchen, are calm and less prone to panic. The rush of the kitchen does not affect them, they work hard and straight through without the afternoon break but have no direct contact with the waitresses. Raymond is emotional. Paul is suave though not unpleasant.

CHEF: A large man of about fifty-nine with a tiny moustache. If he could he would work elsewhere – preferably not in the catering trade at all. The less that is brought to his attention, the happier he feels. In such a large kitchen the organization carries itself almost automatically. He rarely speaks to anyone except Frank, the Second Chef, Max who works near him, and Nicholas who is immediately under him. He will not say good morning or communicate any of the politeness expected of a chef. Familiarity, for him, breeds the contempt it deserves.

MR MARANGO, *Proprietor:* An old man of seventy-five, stout – but not fat – with flabby jowls and a sad expression on his face. A magnificent curtain of grey hair skirts the back of his bald head and curls under itself. His sad look is really one of self-pity. The machine he has set in motion is his whole life and he suspects that everyone is conspiring to stop it.

THE ACTIONS OF THE COOKS

For the purposes of the action of this play the following dishes have been allotted to the cooks. Of course they cannot go through all the actions necessary for the cooking of these dishes. The two important things are:

1. That they have some actions to mime throughout the play in between speaking their parts and gossiping among themselves; and

2. That by the time the service is ready to begin they have an assortment of neatly arranged trays and pots of 'dishes and sauces' ready to serve to the waitresses as requested.

FRANK: Roast pheasant – chips. Roast chicken – pommes sauté. Mushrooms. Pour salt in twenty chicken carcasses; place in oven. Slice carrots and onions and boil for gravy. Salt and place pheasants in oven. (Both carcasses are cleaned eslewhere.) Chop mushrooms and fry together with sauté.

ALFREDO: Roast veal – spaghetti. Boiled ham – boiled potatoes. Roast beef for staff. Season and cook veal and beef in oven. Boil spaghetti in salt water. Chop onions and carrots and make sauce. Place ham in pot to boil.

HANS: Sausages – baked rice. Pork chops – white beans. Vegetables for the staff. Cut up ham, tomatoes, onions, and mushrooms, and sauté for rice. Boil white beans. Pork chops are fried during service. Collect from cold cupboard and heat yesterday's vegetables for staff.

PETER: Mixed fish – sauce. Cod meunière – boiled potatoes. Boiled turbot – sauce hollandaise. Beat egg yellows on slow heat; add melted margarine for sauce hollandaise. This takes a long time. Slice cod and turbot into portions. Slice lemons for garniture.

KEVIN: Grilled sardines – boiled potatoes. Grilled salmon – boiled potatoes. Fried plaice – chips or potatoes. Slice lemons for plaice. Cut salmon into portions. Arrange four trays on bench; one for oil, one for milk, one for flour, and one with required fish. Clean grill with wire brush.

GASTON: Grilled chops – chips. Grilled steak – chips. Most of his work is done during service. Clean grill with wire brush. Collect from veg. room and then blanch chips. Aid Kevin.

MICHAEL: Hamburger – egg on top – chips. Ham omelette. Onion soup. Cut ham for omelette. Cube stale bread for onion soup. Crack eggs in tin ready for omelette. We assume enough soup left over from yesterday.

MAX: Mainly carting of huge meat carcasses from coldroom to bench where he then proceeds to cut and dissect them.

NICHOLAS: Cold roast beef – potato salad. Cold ham – Russian salad. Slice meats and arrange various trays of salad. Also roll and slice in portions chopped meat for Michael's hamburgers.

CHEF: Mainly clerical and organizational work of course. He will mind his own business as much as possible.

PAUL AND RAYMOND: Bands of apple and pear tart. Pastry called 'religieuse'. First bake trays of tarts prepared day before. Spread custard sauce and then slice fruit to lay on top. Make more pastry. Mix flour and fat, add water, roll out. Cut into more bands ready for tomorrow. Fill pastry with cream from cloth bag. Peel fruit.

BERTHA: Hitherto unmentioned because part is small. She is the *veg. cook*. Assume all her vegs., sprouts, cabbage, spinach, and sauté, were cooked day before. She merely has to heat them over. Otherwise gossips with coffee woman.

NOTE: Cooks are continually moving between stations and plate room in order to get pots and pans for cooking in.

Any producer is at liberty to abstract this set if he can also get over the atmosphere.

PETER'S SONG

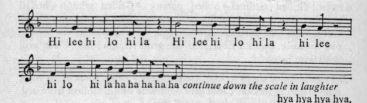

Hi lee hi lo hi la Hi lee hi lo hi la hi lee

hi lo hi la ha ha ha ha ha *continue down the scale in laughter*
hya hya hya hya.

ACT ONE

There is no curtain to this act. The kitchen is always there. It is in semi-darkness. A figure is seen sleeping by the oven. Nothing happens until the audience is quite seated (at the usual time for commencement that is).

[*The figure rises. It is the night porter,* MAGI. *He stretches, looks at his watch, and then stands still, realizing where he is. It is seven in the morning. He switches on a light which just barely lights the kitchen. Then with a burning (?) sheet of paper in his hand he lights the ovens. Into the first shoots a flame. There is smoke and flame, and soon the oven settles into a steady burn and with it comes its hum. It is the hum of the kitchen, a small roar. It is a noise that will stay with us to the end. As he lights each oven the noise grows from a small to a loud ferocious roar. There will be this continuous battle between the dialogue and the noise of the ovens. The producer must work out his own balance.*

The porter exits. Some seconds later he returns with a hefty woman. They are pushing a chariot on which are two cauldrons of potatoes. They lift these on to the oven. 'The spuds,' mutters the woman. They exit and as they do MAX *passes them on his way in. 'Good morning,' he says. He makes his way to his corner, switches on his light, pulls out the drawer beneath his table, and places his belongings in it. At the same time he takes out a bottle of beer, opens it, and drinks. Then he goes to his coldroom offstage and drags out another vat filled with beef. This he hauls to Alfredo's station. Meanwhile the night porter and the hefty woman return with another cauldron of spuds. They hoist it on to the oven.*]

HEFTY WOMAN: There.

MAX [*to Magi*]: Magi, give us a hand, please.

[*They raise the beef on to Alfredo's oven. As they do this* PAUL *and* RAYMOND *enter with their tools under their arms. They go to their own corner and switch on their lights and electric oven.*]

PAUL [*to anybody*]: Good morning, good morning, good morning. [*to Max*] And to you too, Max.

MAX [*his soul not yet returned*]: Good morning.

RAYMOND: Max, it's escallop of veal on . . . today.

MAX: How many?

RAYMOND: Three. I'll take them now and put them in my box, before the others get here.

[MAX *goes to the coldroom and returns with three escallops which he slaps down on his table and* RAY *collects.*]

MAX: And don't forget my puff pastry tomorrow.

RAYMOND: Usual?

MAX: Usual.

PAUL [*to Ray as he returns*]: It's religieuse today?

RAYMOND: Yes. But you do the fruit bands. Leave the pastries, I'll do them.

[*A woman enters from the dining room with a glass stand in her hand. This is* ANNE, *the dessert woman.*]

PAUL: Good morning, Anne.

RAYMOND: Good morning, sweetheart.

ANNE [*Irish, pretty, thirty-five, speaks with slow, cloying lilt*]: Hello, boys, hello, Max.

MAX [*his soul returned*]: Top o' the mornin' to you, Anne.

ANNE [*putting coffee in metal jug to warm on oven*]: An' the rest o' the day to yersel', dear. [*Stretching herself*] Ah, me bed was lovely.

RAYMOND [*lasciviously*]: I bet it was.

ANNE: Hey, Raymond, tell me, what happened to Peter in the end, you know, last night?

RAYMOND: Now he's a silly boy, eh? Don't you think so? I don't even know what it was all about anyway. You know, Paul?

PAUL: All I know is he had a fight with Gaston. Why? I don't know. Over a ladle I think, or maybe a . . .

MAX: He's a bloody German, a fool, that's what he is. He is always quarrelling, always. There's no one he hasn't quarrelled with, am I right? No one! That's some scheme that is, exchanging cooks!

What do we want to exchange cooks for? Three years he's been
here – three years!

ANNE: Ah, the boy's in love.

RAYMOND: What love! You ever see him? When Monique does a
turn as hostess by the stairs he watches her through that mirror
there. [*Points to glass partition.*] And he walks round the kitchen and
looks to see if she's talking or flirting with any of the customers.
You don't believe me?

PAUL: And they quarrel in front of everybody as well. They shout at
each other. Shout! You know, sometimes she doesn't even look
at him and waits for her orders with her back turned.

ANNE: The poor boy. He's no parents you know. But what happened
last night? I want to know.

MAX: Ask Magi.

[MAGI *is the night porter. He is a Cypriot. He has dressed himself
now and is ready to go.*]

MAGI: Any coffee, Anne?

ANNE: Sure dear. [*Pours.*]

RAYMOND: Hey Magi, what happened with Peter last night, uh?

MAGI [*unconcerned*]: They nearly killed him.

ANNE: Oh no!

MAGI: He talk a lot and get away. 'Everyone for me,' he say, 'is the
same. It makes no difference,' he say. A very lucky boy, I tell you.

RAY [*gesticulating*]: But what was it all about, tell me? I don't know
nothing, me.

MAGI: Well, *you* should know that – I wasn't here.

PAUL: All we know is that they suddenly started shouting at each
other. And you know Peter, always shouts more than the other,
and you can always hear Peter – well, so then it stopped, and then
a few seconds later they were fighting and I saw Gaston raise a
pallet knife and Peter knock it out of his hand, and then . . .

RAYMOND: And then he lifted Gaston up and nearly sat him on the
stove and . . .

PAUL: And then the chef came along and . . .

ANNE: Well, *I* saw the chef separate them and I heard Gaston say, 'I haven't finished yet, it's not over yet,' but I still don't know what it was all about.

PAUL: Who cares? I say good morning to Peter but never good night.

MAGI: Well, I came in at nine last night. The boys were changing and suddenly Peter comes and Gaston follows him. Gaston says Peter called him a lousy Cypro and the boys make circle round him and want to murder him! All of them, they all wanted to hit him! And he was scared! I never seen him so white.

ANNE: But what was it about to begin with?

MAX: A ladle, I tell you.

PAUL: Who knows? There's always fights. Who knows how they begin?

MAGI [*laying down cup*]: He was a lucky boy, I tell you. Well, I'm going.

ANNE: And I must get started too. [*Looks round empty kitchen.*] You wouldn't think this place will become a madhouse in two hours would you now? [*Moves off with* MAGI.]

[RAY, PAUL, *and* MAX *continue to work in silence.*]

MAX: Any luck on the pools, Ray?

RAY: Huh!

MAX: Norwich and Leyton let me down. Twenty points. Twenty points!

[*Pause.*]

PAUL: Read about the man in the mental home who won £35,000?

RAY: And his wife turned up after eighteen years?

PAUL: Eighteen years!

[*Pause.* DIMITRIOS *enters – a Cypriot kitchen porter, young, good-looking, and intelligent. He is carrying in his hand a home-made portable record player. He is happy as he takes it to Paul. He speaks with an accent.*]

DIMITRI: I make it, Paul, I make it. There! [*Lays it on table nearby.*] She does not look handsome. I'm sorry for that.

PAUL: Ah, you good boy, Dimitri. Can we play it?

[*He looks round to see if authority is in sight. Only two young waitresses approach. One has a bucket in her hand and her hair is tied up with a scarf. The other one is similarly attired and carries a feather duster.*]

Any one around?

FIRST WAITRESS [*pointing to portable*]: What is it, Paul?

PAUL: Is Marango around yet?

SECOND WAITRESS: Not yet. Whose is it?

PAUL: It's mine. Dimitri here made it.

RAYMOND: You made it on your own? All those little wires and plugs? Tell me, what are you doing here? Why you waste your time with dishes in this place? You can't get a job in a factory?

DIMITRI: A factory? You think I find happiness in a factory? What I make there? Uh? This little wire, you see it? This I would make, or that what you call it . . .

PAUL: Knob.

DIMITRI: Knob. That perhaps I could put in. All day I would screw in knobs. I tell you, in a factory a man makes a little piece till he becomes a little piece, you know what I mean?

FIRST WAITRESS [*stupidly*]: Yeah, he's right you know.

DIMITRI: Sure I know, my brother, he works there. I know all right.

RAYMOND: Hey, Dimitri, *you* know what happened to Peter last night?

DIMITRI: They nearly kill him. Why?

SECOND WAITRESS: Oh, my Gawd.

DIMITRI: But you think it was all Peter's fault? They all wanted to fight. Listen, you put a man in the plate room all day, he's got dishes to make clean and stinking bins to take away and floors to sweep, what else there is for him to do – he wants to fight. He got to show he is a man someway. So – blame him!

PAUL: I got a record with me – can we play it?

DIMITRI: Sure.

[*They plug in the pick-up and play a rock 'n' roll tune.* PAUL *takes a waitress and begins to dance. The other waitress tries to persuade* DIMITRI *to dance but he is shy and will not, so she hops on her own till some others come from the dining room and they either dance or clap their hands. After some seconds a waitress rushes in and cries out* 'Marango is in the dining room.' *There is a scramble to restore everything to normal: work is resumed,* PAUL *puts away the pick-up, and* DIMITRI *vanishes into the plate room.*

Enter ALFREDO.]

ALFREDO: Good morning, gentlemen.

MAX [*pointing to Alfredo's station*]: The veal is there.

ALFREDO [*studying the menu on the board*]: Thank you, thank you.

PAUL [*shouting*]: Is the new cook here?

ALFREDO [*shrugging his shoulders*]: He didn't ask for me.

[*At this point* GASTON *enters first and goes to his station. A few seconds later* MICHAEL *comes in and sets out his business, to be followed by* HANS *who escorts* KEVIN. *Sooner or later they all arrive to glance at the menu on the board.*]

HANS [*to Kevin*]: I not know where you work. On fish perhaps. [*To Paul*] Paul, new cook.

PAUL: Hello.

[*They continue to work while* KEVIN *watches them and the rest of the kitchen.*]

KEVIN: Is there much doing here?

PAUL: You'll see. Two thousand customers a day.

[*While* KEVIN *has been introduced and is talking to the pastrycooks,* BERTHA *has entered. She goes to the cold cupboard and after looking around inside takes out a tray of sliced cold potatoes. Following behind about to start his work is* NICHOLAS. *He has a bottle of beer in his hand which he is drinking.*]

NICK [*to Bertha*]: Where you go with that?

BERTHA: I need it for sauté.

NICK [*taking tray*]: Oh, no, no, no, no. That's for me. Me, I prepared that yesterday. That's for me, for my salad.

BERTHA [*trying to hold on to tray*]: You get your salad from the veg. room.

NICK: Ah no, bloody hell! You get *yours* from the veg. room. That is for me, that is what I get ready.

BERTHA [*nastily*]: You don't bloody hell me, my son. You bloody hell in your own country. [*To others*] What d'you think of him, eh? the little . . .

NICK: This is my country.

BERTHA: The lavatory is your country.

NICK [*taking tray eventually*]: The lavatory is *your* country, and the sewers, you know that? The sewers!

BERTHA [*taking out another tray*]: I'll pay you, sonny. You cross me once, that's all, just once. Lousy little foreigner, you!

NICK [*cheekily*]: For her I'm gonna starve. Listen to her . . .

ALFREDO [*approaching cupboard for his own goods*]: Excuse me, friends, you can carry on in a minute. [*But the quarrel has died down.*]

NICK [*approaching pastry section*]: D'you hear her? Uh? The cow! Paul, you got some tart or cake or something? I'm starving. [PAUL *hands him tart. To Kevin*] You the new cook?

KEVIN: Yes.

NICK: Good luck to you! [*Laughs to the others.*] You know where your station is?

KEVIN: I don't even know what stations there are.

NICK: Here, I'll show you. [*Takes him over to right of stage.*] Well, at the end there, you see that fat bitch? [*Points.*] She's a veg. cook. And next to her we got the second chef, Frank, on poultry; and then Alfredo on the roast; and Hans he does staff and rice and cutlets and you know; and – oh yes, that's the menu. The chef, he writes it out each night. And there is where Peter works, boiled fish and all that. He's not here yet. And over there . . .

[*By this time he has to take Kevin back to left of stage and points out the other stations. As he talks on,* PETER *enters in a great hurry. He is late. He laughs his laugh.*]

PETER: Hya, hya, hya . . . *auf geht's, auf geht's.*

HANS: *Auf geht's, mein Lieber! Was hat dich zurückgehalten heute früh?*

PETER: *Ach, die Frau, die Frau.*

NICK: Peter, the new cook. I give him to you.

PETER: So what shall I do with him? [*To Kevin*] You know where it is you work?

KEVIN: Not yet I don't.

PETER: What restaurant you work in before?

KEVIN: Parisito, Shaftesbury Avenue.

PETER [*rubbing his thumb and finger together*]: Good pay?

KEVIN [*shaking his head*]: That's why I came here.

PETER: Oh, you get good money here – but you work! [*Raising his hands in despair*] Oh, yes! Now, you help me. Can you make a sauce hollandaise? You know – eggs and – [*Makes motion of whisking.*]

KEVIN: Yes, yes.

PETER [*briskly*]: The eggs are already in a tin in the cold cupboard. There is a pot, the whisk is in the drawer and I melt margarine for you.

[*By now almost everybody is working. Waitresses are making an appearance; they are carrying glasses back and forth. One waitress is handing out the printed menu for the day, another is taking round bread for lunch for the kitchen staff. As she reaches the pastrycooks, HANS approaches her shyly and tries to flirt with her. She rebukes his advances and moves off up right stage. FRANK, the second chef, enters and kisses her as she passes. He approaches cold cupboard out of which he takes a bottle of beer.*]

MAX [*to Frank*]: We got no lamb cutlets.

FRANK: Three carcasses came in yesterday.

MAX: So?

FRANK: So!

MAX: So you come and help me cut them up. I'm on my own today.

FRANK: What you got?

MAX: Veal cutlets.

FRANK: O.K., so veal cutlets then. [*Moving to Kevin.*] New cook?

KEVIN [*sweating and still beating his sauce*]: Yes, Chef.

FRANK: Right, you work on the fried fish this morning.

PETER [*approaching from cutting table*]: Thank you, thank you; but I got six dishes to prepare.

FRANK: Co-Co is off today. Someone must do the fry.

PETER: Bloody house this is. The middle of summer and we got no staff. I got six dishes.

[FRANK *takes* KEVIN *to the friture and leaves* GASTON *to explain what has to be done. The* CHEF *enters now. He walks straight to his table, ignoring* HANS *who says 'Good morning, Chef.'* FRANK *approaches him, talks a while, and then returns to his own station. Meanwhile –*]

HANS [*to Peter*]: *Er hat dich beinahe erwischt gestern Abend.*

PETER: *Nur zusammen sind sie mutig.*

HANS: *Haben sie nicht für dich draussen gewartet?*

PETER: *Ja, da waren einige, aber ich war zusammen mit Monika. Ha! jetzt spricht sie nicht mehr mit. Ach, nun – auf geht's!* [*Sings his song, in which* HANS *joins him, ending in laughter.*]

PETER: Hey, Gaston. I'm sorry – your black eye, I'm sorry about it.

GASTON: DON'T TALK TO ME.

PETER: I say I'm sorry, that's all.

GASTON: You sorry because half a dozen Cypriot boys make you feel sorry – but we not finished yet!

PAUL: Gaston! What's the matter with you? A man is saying sorry – so accept!

GASTON: Accept? He give me this [*pointing to black eye*] and I must accept? [*To Peter*] We not finished yet I'm telling you.

PETER: What you not finished with? Tell me! What you want to do now? You want to give me a black eye? That make you feel happier? All right! Here, give me one and then we'll be finished, eh? [*Adopts quixotic stance.*]

GASTON: Don't laugh, Peter. I'm telling you, it gets worse, don't laugh.

[PETER *adopts another quixotic stance.*]

PAUL [*to Peter*]: So what are you tantalizing him for? Lunatic! [*To Raymond*] Nobody knows when to stop. A quarrel starts and it goes on for months. When one of them *is* prepared to apologize so the other doesn't know how to accept – and when someone knows *how* to accept so the other . . . ach! Lunatics. [*Throws a hand of disgust.*]

FRANK [*shouting from his station to Nick*]: Nicholas! Twelve chickens, please.

NICK [*looking in cupboard*]: There is only six here.

FRANK: Well, order some more, then.

HANS [*joining in the shouting*]: *Auf geht's*, Nicholas, come on, Nicholas. [*At this point* RAYMOND *passes on way to plate room.*] *Buon giorno, Raymondo. Come state?*

RAYMOND: *Bene, bene, grazie. Su con il lavoro!*

HANS: *Una lunga vita ai lavoratori!*

MAX [*suddenly and violently to Hans*]: You're in England now, speak bloody English. [HANS *is nonplussed for the day.*] Everybody speaking in a different language, French, Italian, German. [*To Hans*] You came here to learn English, didn't you? Well, speak it then!

PETER: What's the matter, Max? You frightened of something? Have another beer.

MAX: I'm not frightened of you, I tell you that straight. So *you* can keep quiet.

PETER [*approaching close to Max and talking in his ear*]: You know your trouble, Max? You been here too long.

MAX [*moving away from him*]: Yes, yes, yes, Peter, all right.

PETER [*following him*]: How long have you been here? Twenty-one years? You need a change.

MAX [*moving away again*]: Yes, yes.

PETER [*following him*]: Why don't you go work a season in Germany?

MAX: Sure to.

PETER: Visit other kitchens? Learn more!

MAX: Yes, yes. Get on with your work.

PETER: Don't you worry about my work.

HANS: *Ach verlass ihn.*

PETER: You can't bear a change, can you? A new face upsets you.

MAX: Let's drop it, uh? Enough, yes?

HANS: *Es lohnt sich nicht, mein Lieber.*

CHEF: All right, Peter, let's have some work, yes?

[*PETER returns to his work and winks at Raymond in passing. Now* MR MARANGO *enters. He is walking slowly round the kitchen, inspecting everything, placing his hand on the hot-plate to see if it is still working. It is a mechanical movement – sometimes he puts a hand on the cold pastry slab to see if it is still hot – it is a mechanical tour. Meanwhile –*]

KEVIN [*to Peter*]: Is it like this every day? [*Wiping sweat from forehead.*] Look at me, I never sweated so much since me glorious honeymoon.

PETER: It is nothing this. This is only how it begins. Wait till we start serving, then! [*Raises his hands.*] You in place?

KEVIN: More or less. I got me salmon to cut.

PETER: Good, we eat soon.

MARANGO [*gently to Kevin*]: You're the new cook?

KEVIN [*wiping his brow again*]: Yes, sir.

MARANGO: It's hot, eh, son?

KEVIN: Sure, an'a bit more.

MARANGO: Never mind, I pay you well. Just work, that's all, just work well. [*Continues tour.*]

KEVIN [*to Peter*]: He seems a kind old man.

PETER: You think he is kind? He is a bastard! He talks like that because it is summer now. Not enough staff to serve all his customers, that is why he is kind. You going to stay till winter? Wait till then, you'll see. The fish is burnt! Too much mis-en-place! The soup is sour! He is not a man, he is a restaurant, I tell you. He goes to market at five-thirty in the morning; returns here, reads the mail, goes up to the office, and then comes down here to watch the service. Here he stands, sometimes he walks round touching the hot-plate, closing the hot-plate doors, looking inside this thing and that thing. Till the last customer he stays. Then he has a sleep upstairs in his office. Half an hour after we come back he is here again, till nine-thirty, maybe ten at night. Every day, morning to night. What kind of a life is that, in a kitchen! Is that a life, I ask you? Me, I don't care, soon I'm going to get married and then whisht – [*Makes movement with his arm to signify 'I'm off'*.]

HANS [*approaches with large tray in his hand which he later puts in cold cupboard*]: Auf geht's, Irishman. I must not speak German to you. This is England, Irishman. [*Loudly as he moves off.*] Auf geht's, hya, hya, hya.

[*At this point* MONIQUE *passes by where Peter is working. She is Peter's girl, a pretty, petite blonde. Really she is a waitress, but today is the Hostess's day off and she takes over. She is carrying glasses. All she says to Peter is 'Bully'. They have been quarrelling.*]

PETER [*to Monique*]: Go to hell! [*To Kevin proudly*] That's my wife or she will be soon. Look – [*takes out card from wallet*] – this card she sent me when she was on holiday. [*Reading aloud.*] 'I am not happy till you come. I love you very much.' And look, her lipstick marks. She is very lovely, yes?

KEVIN: She looks like a girl I knew, all bosom and bouncing, you know?

PETER [*not really understanding what Kevin said*]: We eat soon, eh? [KEVIN *goes off to peruse his printed menu. To Hans*] Hans, hilf' mir. [*They take a large, heavy pot off the oven and pass the contents through a strainer into a small pot which* PETER *has prepared on the ground.*]

KEVIN [*showing menu to Peter*]: Look here, it says on the printed menu fried plaice and on the board it says fried sole.

PETER: See the chef.

KEVIN [*approaching chef*]: Good morning, Chef. Look, it says here fried plaice and on the board it's got fried sole.

CHEF: I don't know anything about it, it was my day off yesterday. See the second chef.

KEVIN: Have we got any plaice?

CHEF [*sarcastically looking inside his apron*]: It's not here.

KEVIN [*moves away to Raymond*]: Now that's a helpful person for you. Doesn't he care about anything?

RAYMOND: He don't want to know nothing, only when it's gone wrong.

[MONIQUE *again passes in front of Peter to glasserie.* PETER *is angry. Tries to make his quarrel secret, but of course this is impossible.*]

PETER: Why do you still call me bully, all day you call me bully.

MONIQUE [*moves away across front of stage*]: Bully!

PETER [*following her and talking, as is his habit, in her ear*]: You think to make me angry? What is it you wanted me to do? Let him fight me?

MONIQUE [*turning to him at last*]: He's got a black eye now, you see?

PETER: I see, I see. But he raised a knife to me.

MONIQUE: Bully. [*She turns away.*]

PETER [*following her like the pathetic, jealous lover*]: And remember, you're hostess today. I can see you in the glass. No flirting, do you hear? [*Grips her arm.*] No flirting.

MONIQUE: I shall talk to who I like. [*Moves off.*]

PETER [*hoping no one can hear him*]: Cow! Disgusting cow! All the restaurant can see you.

[*At this point* HANS *draws out the table from the pastry section more to the centre of the stage and begins to lay it with cutlery and glasses and bread ready for lunch.* ALFREDO *also lays himself a place on the counter between where* PETER *and* HANS *work.* MAX, NICHOLAS, *and* FRANK *prepare to eat at Max's table.* KEVIN, MICHAEL, PETER, *and* HANS *will eat at the table* HANS *is now laying.* GASTON *will not eat because he will not sit with* PETER. *These two continue to ignore each other throughout the day.*]

MICHAEL [*shouting*]: Who has the strainer? Gaston? Peter?

PETER: I got it here, you'll have to clean it. [*To a kitchen porter who is nearby.*] Hey, Mangolis, you clean this for Michael, please?

[MANGOLIS *makes a rude sign with his hand and moves off.* PETER *shrugs his shoulders and* MICHAEL *heaves up strainer himself and carts it off. A waitress stops in her work to speak to Peter.*]

WAITRESS [*as though she wants him to confide in her only*]: Hey, Peter, what happened last night? They didn't . . .

PETER [*briskly, she only wants to gossip*]: No, no. Cowards all of them. It was nothing.

PAUL [*to same waitress as she passes his section*]: Hettie, did you go last night?

HETTIE [*ecstatically*]: Mmm.

PAUL: He's a good actor?

HETTIE [*even more ecstatically and hugging herself*]: What a man! I simply melt – oh, one night, just one night with him and then I wash dishes all my life. [*Moves off.*]

RAYMOND [*to Paul*]: So what chance do we stand? You wonder my wife doesn't make love like she used to?

PAUL: And that's why I'm not going to get married. I buy picture books and I'm happy.

WAITRESS: All right, boys, staff meal coming up.

[*While* PAUL *and* RAYMOND *are talking, a long procession of straggling, gossiping, and giggling waitresses have come down stage on the left and are moving around in front of Peter's station and up the other side to* HANS *and* ALFREDO *who have laid trays of food on the serving counter. Beside food are piles of plates. The waitresses help themselves.*]

FIRST WAITRESS: What've you got for us this morning?

ALFREDO: Curried cats and dogs.

SECOND WAITRESS: Is this cabbage from yesterday?

HANS: It's all right, it's all right, eat it, eat.

THIRD WAITRESS: What are these?

HANS: Very good, very good. Cauliflower and white sauce.

FOURTH WAITRESS: White sauce? It smells.

FIFTH WAITRESS: Got anything good, Hans?

HANS: If you don't like, go to chef.

SIXTH WAITRESS: Got any boiled potatoes?

HANS: Not cooked yet, not ready, ach. . . .

[HANS *moves away in disgust leaving them to serve themselves. He watches Peter working a second and then goes into steam room. As the waitresses are serving themselves and grumbling and eventually moving off to the dining room, we discover that* NICHOLAS *has been arguing with a very tall and heavily made-up waitress near to the glasserie. He is making his quarrel much too public for her liking. He is probably a little drunk already.*]

NICK [*urging her*]: Come with me and ask him. Come on.

WAITRESS: No Nicky, no – now stop.

NICK: Well, why don't you believe me then? If I tell you I got to stay the afternoon why don't you believe me? [*Shouting*] Frank! Frank! Where is he now? [*Wanders off in search of Frank while waitress waits wondering what he is going to do.*]

RAYMOND [*shouting to waitress*]: Hit him! Go on, you're big enough. [*Nudges* PAUL, *they laugh.*]

FRANK [*as he is dragged into the scene by* NICHOLAS]: What do you want me for? What is it now, eh?

WAITRESS: Oh, Nicky, don't be a fool. [*To Ray and Paul despairingly*] Oh, for Christ's sake, what do you think of him now?

NICK: No, ask him, go on. You don't believe me.

FRANK: Ask him what for hell's sake?

NICK: Have I got to work in the afternoon or haven't I?

FRANK [*moving away incredulous that he has been called away for this*]: You called me for *that*? You mad or something? Do me a favour and leave me out of this will you. [*Grinning to the others*] Asks me to solve his marriage problems. [*To Nick*] I'll tell you how to do it as well, ha, ha, ha!

[*Crashing in on laughter is a loud scream from the steam room.* HANS *comes running out with his hands covering his face. He curses in German:* 'Zum Kuckuck noch mal! Verdammt! Zum Teufel!' *A number of people run and crowd him.*]

FRANK: What is it, Hans?

HANS: Who bloody fool put a pot of hot water on steamer?

PETER: It fell on you?

HANS [*moving away from crowd*]: Bastard house! I never worked before so bad. Never, never . . . [PETER *takes him away for some first aid.*]

A WAITRESS [*calling after them*]: Put some of that yellow stuff on him.

FRANK: He'll live. [*To the crowd*] All right, it's all over, come on. [*Crowd disperses,* FRANK *moves to Chef.*] No matter how many times you tell them they still rush around.

CHEF [*he is not interested, shrugs shoulders*]: Is the new chap all right?

FRANK: He seems to be. Look out. [MARANGO *approaches.*]

MARANGO: What happened to the boy?

CHEF [*as though concerned*]: I don't know. I wasn't there. Frank, what happened?

FRANK [*wearily*]: Someone left a pot of boiling water on one of the steamers and he tipped it over his face.

MARANGO: He's burnt his face. It's not serious [*to Chef*] but it might have been. [*He shakes his head sadly and moves away.*]

CHEF: What can I do, Mr Marango? They rush about like mad, I tell them but they don't listen.

[MARANGO *moves off, shaking his head still.*]

CHEF [*to Frank*]: Much he cares! It interrupts the kitchen so he worries. Three more years, Frank, three, that's all and then whisht! retire, finish! Then you can take over.

FRANK: Oh no! Not this boy. I'm in charge one day a week – enough! They can find another madman.

CHEF: Do you think I'm mad?

FRANK: Do you enjoy your work?

CHEF: Who cares?

FRANK: So on top of not enjoying your work you take on responsibility – that isn't mad?

CHEF: I've got a standard of living to keep up – idiot!

FRANK [*moving off*]: So go mad!

[PETER *and* HANS *return.* HANS' *face is now a curious red and yellow.* KEVIN *and* PAUL *go up to them.*]

KEVIN: You all right?

[HANS *makes a movement of his hands to say 'Ach, I'm fed-up, forget it.'*]

PAUL: You look beautiful.

KEVIN: A Red Indian.

PETER: Come on, let's eat.

[*They all move to their places to eat.* PAUL *returns to his work. There is less activity in the kitchen now, the calm before the storm. A few waitresses wander around, a porter sweeps the floor.*]

KEVIN [*to Peter*]: How long have you been here?

PETER: Three years.

KEVIN: How did you stick it?

MICHAEL: Sick already?

KEVIN: I don't think I'll last the day.

PETER: People are always coming and going.

HANS [*he is not eating much*]: I think me I'll go soon.

MICHAEL [*to Kevin*]: The worse is to come. [*To others*] Am I right? You wait till the service, ah . . . But you'll get used to it after a while.

PETER: We all said we wouldn't last the day, but tell me what is there a man can't get used to? Nothing! You just forget where you are and you say it's a job.

MICHAEL: He should work on the eggs. Five dishes I've got, five! Hey, Paul, any cakes?

PAUL: They're all gone – I got some tart from yesterday. [*Raising his shoulders*] Sorry!

PETER [*not too loudly*]: Liar!

KEVIN: I thought you could eat what you liked here.

MICHAEL: You can, but you have to swipe it. Even the door for cooking. If I want to make an onion soup that's any good I go to the coldroom and I take some chicken's wings to make my stock. No questions, just in and out – whisht!

HANS: I think I go to America.

KEVIN: America?

HANS [grins sheepishly, he is about to surprise Kevin]: I been to New York already.

KEVIN: You have?

HANS: I already been twice. [Nods head to say 'what do you think of that!'] Worked on a ship. [Pause.] On a ship you waste more than you eat. [Lets this sink in.] You throw everything into the sea before you come on land. [Sinks in further.] Whole chickens! The gulls, you know, they eat it.

KEVIN: What about New York?

HANS [kissing his fingers]: The Empire State Buildings . . . ! And Broadway, Broadway – you heard of Broadway? [KEVIN nods with his mouth full.] Ah . . . Beautiful city.

KEVIN: I heard it, yes.

HANS [in his stride now. Grimace, meaning – no question of it!]: Three in the morning, you know? Women! Night clubs! Rush here, rush there. [More grimace. Secretly] This house not very good here.

KEVIN: It's not, eh?

PETER: You got to turn out food hot and quickly. Quality – pooh! No time!

KEVIN: Even in the small restaurants they're not after caring much.

MICHAEL [lighting cigarette]: Why should they! It's this [rubs thumb and finger together] that counts, you know that.

KEVIN: Oh, I don't know. You'd've thought it was possible to run a small restaurant that could take pride in its food and make money too.

PETER: Of course it's possible, my friend – but you pay to eat in it. It's money. It's all money. The world chase money so you chase money too. [Snapping his fingers in a lunatic way] Money! Money! Money! [An idea] Aha! Watch, watch how Frank hates me.

[PETER picks up a glass with water in it and moves gently to where FRANK eats. His back is to Peter. PETER places glass in the cup of Frank's tall white hat and creeps back laughing his laugh to himself.

FRANK *of course moves and the water spills over him. More laughter from Peter.*]

FRANK [*shouting across to him*]: One day you'll lay an egg too many and it'll crack under you. Yes – you laugh.

PETER: Frank is also unhappy. [*Waitress approaches table.*] Yes?

WAITRESS [*lays hand on Michael's shoulders; he lays his on her buttocks*]: Who's on fish today?

MICHAEL: Do you love me?

WAITRESS: I think you're irresistible. Who's on fish?

KEVIN: Me.

WAITRESS: Right, I order four plaice. [*Moves off.*]

PETER [*easing Kevin back to seat because he has just risen to serve that order*]: You got time. You not finished your lunch yet. The customer can wait. [*To Kevin*] Be like Mr Alfredo. Nothing disturbs Mr Alfredo. Mr Alfredo is a worker and he hates his boss. He knows his job but he does no more no less and at the right time. Mr Alfredo is an Englishman – look!

[*At this point* MR ALFREDO *comes to the front of the stage and looks around to see no one is watching. No one is. He tucks something first into the right of his apron, then, still looking to see no one has seen, he tucks something into the left of his apron. Then straightening himself out he returns to pick his teeth. A waitress approaches Frank.*]

WAITRESS: Mr Marango wants a leg of chicken and some sauté.

FRANK: Mr Marango can go to hell, I'm eating.

WAITRESS [*moves off*]: I'll call for it in five minutes.

FRANK: They don't give you a chance to eat here.

MAX: Hey, you heard they nearly killed Peter last night?

FRANK: Don't talk to me about that boy. He's mad. I've had too much of him already. . . . Three years.

NICK: They should kill 'em off! Kill 'em off! The lot! Bosch! I hate them you know. I don't hate no one like I hate them. And they want to abolish hanging now. You read about it?

MAX [*to Frank*]: Do you think that Bill 'll go through?

FRANK: How should I know! I suppose it's worth a try.

MAX: They'll be sorry, I'm telling you.

NICK [*self-righteously*]: What I say is, if a man he kills another then he should be killed too.

MAX [*approvingly*]: An eye for an eye.

NICK: And we should use the electric chair. It's no good the hanging.

MAX [*enjoying what he is about to say*]: Remember those two they put on the chair in America not long ago, for spying? The bloody thing misfired – ha – they had to do it again. I bet the electrician on that mob copped out. . . .

[MONIQUE *walks past Peter to front of stage and waits for him by his station. She has a cup of tea in her hand.* PETER *jumps up and goes to her. They do this every meal break.*]

PETER: Where are you going tomorrow?

MONIQUE: Dancing at the Astra.

PETER: Why do you have to go there? All the prostitutes go there.

MONIQUE: I'm going with Monty.

PETER: Listen, Monique. Tell Monty tonight. Ask for a divorce, eh? We can't go on like thieves, we do damage to ourselves, you know that?

MONIQUE: Peter, not here, please. I can't tell him yet.

PETER: Here – inside here [*knocks at his head with his hand*] we do damage. We insult ourselves. I'm not going to wait much longer, you'll see. You think I like this Tivoli? You don't believe me I won't wait do you?

MONIQUE: Please yourself.

PETER [*despairingly*]: What do you want me to do? Do you want to make me something to laugh at? Three years I'm here now, three . . .

[MONIQUE *leaves him, saying* 'Not now.' PETER *is about to become furious but controls himself and as though in high spirits kicks a cardboard margarine box that has been lying around.*]

PETER [*shouting*]: Auf geht's, Irishman. Finish now. Auf geht's.

[PETER *sings his song and* HANS *and* KEVIN *join in with him as they – and indeed all the cooks – clear away their plates and prepare to face the service.* CHEF *approaches Kevin.*]

CHEF: You all right?

KEVIN: Yes, Chef.

CHEF: In place and everything?

KEVIN: Yes, Chef.

[CHEF *moves in to show Kevin how it's done. First dip fish into milk, then flour and the friture.*]

PETER [*to Hans*]: Watch him now, the Irishman. Hya, hya, hya! Soon he won't know what is happening. Watch. Hya, hya, hya!

[*The waitresses begin to enter, shouting their orders at the required station. They take plates from hot-plate, cradle them in their arms, and order. They appear in greater numbers as the service swings into motion. Queues form in front of first one cook, then another.*]

HANS [*shouting to Max*]: Veal cutlets and sausages, please!

MAX: Ye-es. [*Takes them in tray to Hans.*]

GASTON [*shouting to Max*]: Send up the steaks and mutton chops!

MAX [*angrily*]: Wait a bloody minute, will you!

GASTON [*in panic*]: I got six steaks ordered already.

MAX: So what am I supposed to do?

GASTON [*to nobody in particular*]: Everybody the same. I've always got a big queue before I start. [*Returns mumbling.*]

FIRST WAITRESS [*to Kevin*]: Three plaice, please.

KEVIN: Three plaice? Right.

SECOND WAITRESS: Two grilled salmon, do we order it?

KEVIN: Yes, five minutes.

THIRD WAITRESS: Three grilled sardines, please.

KEVIN [*rushing around*]: Right away!

FOURTH WAITRESS: Four plaice, please.

KEVIN: All right, all right.

PETER [*shouting while he serves*]: Ha! ha! Hee! hee! Ho! ho! They're here! They come!

FIRST WAITRESS [*to Peter*]: Two turbot.

PETER: Two turbot!

SECOND WAITRESS: Three dishes of fish.

PETER [*rushing around*]: Three dishes of fish!

THIRD WAITRESS: Are my six cod ready yet?

PETER: When did you order them?

THIRD WAITRESS: Five minutes ago. I came past and you were talking to Hans – remember?

PETER: I remember nothing. Come back in five minutes. Next?

THIRD WAITRESS: You weren't listening, that's what it was.

PETER [*rudely*]: You ordered nothing I say, now come back five minutes' time. Next? [*Next one orders.*]

HANS [*shouting to his waitresses who aren't in a queue*]: You wait yes? You can't see the cutlets cook?

> [*The* CHEF *is wandering around in all this as though he were searching for something further ahead. It is his way of making the cooks believe he is not really watching them. As he stands by the pastry section a* HEAD WAITER *comes up to him.*]

HEAD WAITER: Ten minutes ago Daphne ordered six cod and they are not ready yet.

CHEF [*walks up to Peter*]: The cod – not ready yet?

PETER [*in the midst of his rush*]: She's a liar, you know the one, Chef? She ordered nothing. Here [*hands six cod*].

> [CHEF *passes on cod to* HEAD WAITER *and moves on.* PETER *makes a face after him and when it is safe he begins to sing his song while working. Half-way through he breaks off and rushes to oven. There is something vast and Shakespearian in the way* PETER *moves; he is always wanting to play the fool.*]

PETER: Oh God! She burns! The cod! Hya, hya, hya. She burns, Irishman. No good, no good. [*Rushes the frying-pan with the burnt fish to the dustbin nearby and covers it with paper.*] Ssh, sssssh. Hya, hya, hya.

HANS [*to Peter, loudly, in the midst of his own work*]: That is not too good work, Peter, not good work *mein Lieber*. Pig's work. [*Laughs and points to Kevin who has large queue at his station.*] We have busy time, Irishman, yes?

KEVIN: For God's sake help me. [PETER *rushes to his aid laughing.*]

PETER: Let's go, Irishman, let's go. [*To a waitress.*] The next?

FIRST WAITRESS: Two salmon.

PETER: Right. [*He serves while* KEVIN *replenishes the supply.*] And the next?

SECOND WAITRESS: Three sardines.

PETER: And the next?

> [*He rushes like mad crying, 'And the next, the next!' They each give him their order. Meanwhile* HANS *dashes between his own station and Peter's. The whole tempo of work is speeded up suddenly. Waitresses rush around with dishes in their arms. Porters clear away dirty pots. Orders are being shouted; every station has its share of waitresses. At this moment a queue has formed at Peter's station and he now rushes there laughing like a merry fool going into battle.*]

PETER: Look at this – hya, hya – good morning ladies – and the next. . . .

FIRST WAITRESS [*to Peter*]: Three mixed fish. [PETER *serves her and cries out, 'Next, next', and so on.*]

SECOND WAITRESS: Two cod.

THIRD WAITRESS: One turbot.

FOURTH WAITRESS: One cod.

KEVIN [*to Peter*]: I've run out of lemons!

PETER [*with rude indifference*]: Well, cut some more then. The next?

KEVIN: Let me borrow your cutting board then, please. [*He moves to take it from Peter's bench.*]

PETER [*he stops his work and jumping on* KEVIN *grabs board. In the kitchen it is each man for himself now*]: Oh no, no, no, no, my friend. The plate room, the plate room, in the plate room you'll find them. This is mine, I have need of it.

KEVIN: But I'll give it back in a few seconds.

PETER [*pointing*]: The plate room. [*Slams his hand down on the board for emphasis. To a waitress –*] What do you want?

KEVIN [*surprised at this change in Peter*]: Well, speak a little human like, will yer, please?

PETER: No time, no time.

WAITRESS [*to Peter*]: Will you please serve me with three turbot?

PETER: I've only got two left, in five minutes, five minutes, come back in five minutes. [*Dashes off to steam room to get a new plate of turbot in water ready to boil.*]

    [*Meanwhile* KEVIN *is being harassed at his station. While he is busy cutting up some more lemons a queue of demanding waitresses begin to pester him. As the first waitress calls for her order the* CURTAIN *begins to fall very, very, very slowly so that when it is completely fallen we can still hear Peter cry, 'Auf geht's.'*]

FIRST WAITRESS [*to Kevin*]: Me sole, luvvy, got me sole?

KEVIN: Wait a minute, can yer?

SECOND WAITRESS: You should have it all ready, Paddy, me boy. No time for breathing here. [*She turns for confirmation to her friends who agree.*]

KEVIN [*still rushing around*]: Jesus, is this a bloody madhouse or something? You all gone mad?

    [*The waitresses laugh among themselves, a rather fiendish laughter.*]

THIRD WAITRESS: Come on, Paddy.

PETER [*in the midst of his own rushing*]: Auf geht's, auf geht's. [*He laughs his laugh, and the lights fade on the Kitchen's rush.*]

INTERLUDE

Lights fade up on the sound of a guitar.

It is afternoon break.

The sounds of the oven are at half.

    [PAUL *and* RAYMOND *are working in their corner. These are the only two who stay through the afternoon.*

    KEVIN *is flat out on his back on a wooden bench – exhausted.*

DIMITRI *is slowly sweeping up.*
PETER *is sitting by a table waiting for Monique.*
HANS *is in a corner singing 'Ah sinner-man' in German to a guitar.*]

KEVIN: Finished! I'm done! I'm boiled! You can serve me up for supper!

PAUL [*as if ordering a meal*]: Two portions of boiled Irishman, please! With garnish!

RAYMOND [*also calling*]: Two fried tomatoes on his ears, potatoes round his head, and stuff his mouth with an extra helping of peas.

PAUL: Sprinkle with shamrock and serve with chips – if you please.

KEVIN: I'll produce me own gravy! But did you see it? Did-you-see-that? Fifteen hundred customers and an' half of them eating fish. *I* had to start work on a Friday!

RAYMOND: It's every day the same, my friend.

KEVIN [*raising himself up*]: Look at me. I'm soaking. Look at this jacket. I can wring it out. That's not sweat, no man carries that much water. [*Flopping back again.*] Kevin, you'll drop dead if you stay. I'm warning you, Kevin, take a tip from a friend, hop it! Get out! You've got your youth, Kevin – keep it! This is no place for a human being – you'll drop dead, I'm telling yous.

DIMITRI: Hey, Irishman, what you grumbling about this place for? Is different anywhere else? This stinking kitchen is like the world – you know what I mean? It's too fast to know what happens. People come and people go, big excitement, big noise. [*Makes noise, gesticulates and runs wildly about, and then stops.*] What for? In the end who do you know? You make a friend, you going to be all your life his friend, but when you go from here – pshtt! you forget! Why you grumble about this one kitchen?

PETER: You're a very intelligent boy, Dimitri.

DIMITRI: And you're a bloody fool. I'm sure not I want to talk with you.

KEVIN: Oh, not the Gaston row again. All the morning I hear how Peter give Gaston a black eye. It's the break, no rows, please, it's peace. Can you hear it? It's lovely. It's silence. It's nothing – ahhh! [*Moves.*] Oooh – I'm drowning, in me own sweat. Christ! What a way to die.

DIMITRI [*to Peter*]: A bloody fool you!

[PETER *picks up a cardboard box and puts it over Dimitri's head.* DIMITRI *flings it off angrily and is about to throw it back, but he sees* PETER *with his head in his hands. Instead he takes out a cigarette box and begins rolling Peter a cigarette. He gives the paper to* PETER *to lick, then continues folding it and hands it to him.*]

PETER: Hey, Irishman, I thought you didn't like this place. Why don't you go home and sleep.

KEVIN: Me home is a room and a bed and a painting of the Holy Virgin. It'll always be there.

PETER: Like this place, this house – this too, it'll always be here. That's a thought for you, Irishman. This – this madhouse, it's always here. When you go, when I go, when Dimitri go – this kitchen stays. It'll go on when we die, think about that. We work here – eight hours a day, sweat our guts, and yet – it's nothing. We take nothing. Here – the kitchen, here – you. You and the kitchen. And the kitchen don't mean nothing to you and you don't mean to the kitchen nothing. Dimitri is right, you know – why do you grumble about this kitchen? The world is filled with kitchens – only some they call offices and some they call factories. There, Irishman – what do you say to that?

KEVIN: You want to come in one morning and find it gone?

PETER: Just one morning. Imagine it, eh? Gone. All this gone.

KEVIN: So you'd be out of work!

PETER: So I'd die?

KEVIN: It doesn't worry you, I suppose.

HANS: *Du träumst schon wieder, mein Lieber.*

KEVIN: What's he say?

PETER: He say – I'm dreaming. [*Starts to sing his rowdy 'Hi lee hi lo' song, but stops and lets* HANS *continue his guitaring.*] Hey, Irishman, how do you dream?

KEVIN: How's that?

PETER: Listen, Irishman – I give you a chance to dream – hey Paul, Raymondo, Dimitri – stop work a minute, you got time. Here, come here. [*All but* RAYMOND *gather round.*] We are all given a chance to dream. The ovens are low, the customers gone, Marango is gone, it's all quiet. God has given us a chance now! So dream. Go ahead and dream. Dimitri, you! You dream first.

DIMITRI [*after a pause*]: In this place? With iron around me? And dustbins? And black walls?

PETER: Pretend! The walls are sky, yes? The iron, it's rocks on a coast. The dustbins [*thinks*] they're bushes, and the ovens are the noise of winds. Look at the lights – stars Dimitri.

[*The others gasp and make rude noises at this poetry.*]

HANS: Dreaming, *mein Lieber*, dreaming, dreaming.

PETER [*angrily*]: I want to dream. I feel like it. Dimitri – dream – a little dream, what you see?

DIMITRI [*after a longer pause*]: A little, a little er – what you call it – a small house, sort of –

PAUL: A hut?

DIMITRI: No –

KEVIN: A shed?

DIMITRI: That's right, a shed. With instruments, and tools, and I make lots of radios and television sets maybe, and . . .

PETER: Ach! Silly boy. A hobby he dreams of! Hey, Irishman – you – you dream.

KEVIN: Sleep, me. Most people sleep and dream, me – I dream of sleep!

PETER: Hans – you, what are your dreams?

[HANS *sings on, as though not answering the question. Then –*]

HANS: *Geld! Mein Lieber!* Money. With money I'm a good man, I'm generous, I love all the world. Money, *mein Lieber*, *Geld!* [*Continues to sing.*]

PETER: How can you talk of money, Hans, when you're singing?

HANS: Dreaming, *mein Lieber*, dreaming, dreaming.

PETER: Raymondo?

RAYMOND: Women!

PETER: Paul?

PAUL: Listen, Peter – I'll tell you something. I'm going to be honest with you. You don't mind if I'm honest? Right! I'm going to be honest with you! I don't like you. Now wait a minute, let me finish. I don't like you! I think you're a pig! You bully, you're jealous, you go mad with your work, you always quarrel. All right! But now it's quiet, the ovens are low, the work has stopped for a little, and now I'm getting to know you. I still think you're a pig only now – not so much of a pig. So that's what I dream. I dream of a friend. You give me a rest, you give me silence, you take away this mad kitchen so I make friends, so I think – maybe all the people I thought were pigs are not so much pigs.

PETER: You think people are pigs, eh?

PAUL: Listen, I'll tell you a story. I agree with Dimitri also. The world is filled with kitchens – and when it's filled with kitchens you get pigs. I'll tell you. Next door me, next door where I live is a bus driver. Comes from Hoxton; he's my age, married and got two kids. He says good morning to me; I ask him how he is, I give his children sweets. That's our relationship. Somehow he seems frightened to say too much, you know? God forbid I might ask him for something. So we make no demands on each other. Then one day the busman go on strike. He's out for five weeks. Every morning I say to him, 'Keep going mate, you'll win.' Every morning I give him words of encouragement, I say I understand his cause. I've got to get up earlier to get to work but I don't mind. We're neighbours, we're workers together, he's pleased. I give him money for the strike fund. I can see he's pleased. Then one Sunday, there's a peace march. I don't believe they do much good but I go, because in this world a man's got to show he can still say his piece. The next morning he comes up to me and he says, now listen to this, he says, 'Did you go on that peace march yesterday?' So I says yes, I did go on that peace march yesterday.

So then he turns round to me and he says: 'You know what? A bomb should've been dropped on the lot of them! It's a pity,' he says, 'that they had children with them, 'cos a bomb should've been dropped on the lot!' And you know what was upsetting him? The march was holding up the traffic, the buses couldn't move so fast! Now I don't want him to say I'm right, I don't want him to agree with what I did, but what makes me so sick with terror is that he didn't stop to think that this man helped me in my cause so maybe, only *maybe*, there's something in his cause, I'll talk about it. No! The buses were held up so drop a bomb, he says, on the lot! And you should've seen the hate in his eyes, as if I'd murdered his child. Like an animal he looked. And the horror is this – that there's a wall, a big wall between me and millions of people like him. And I think – where will it end? What do you do about it? And I look around me, at the kitchen, at the factories, at the enormous bloody buildings going up with all those offices and all those people in them and I think Christ! I think. Christ, Christ, Christ! [*He moves round and round with his hand on his head.*] I agree with you, Peter – maybe one morning we should wake up and find them all gone. But then I think: I should stop making pastries? The factory workers should stop making trains and cars? The miner should leave the coal where it is? [*Pause.*] *You* give *me* an answer. You give me your dream.

KEVIN: Hush, patissier! Hush! It's quiet now. Gently now.

[*There is a long silence.* HANS *who had stopped playing now continues. The ovens hum.*]

PETER: I ask for dreams – you give me nightmares.

PAUL: So I've dreamt! Is it my fault if it's a nightmare?

KEVIN: We're waiting for your dream now, Peter boy.

DIMITRI [*jumping up suddenly*]: This is the United Nations, eh? A big conference. Is Russia here, and America and France and England – and Germany too. Is all here. And they got on a competition. Is finished the wars, is finished the rows. Everybody gone home. We got time on our hands. A prize of one million dollars for the best dream. Raymondo, he want a new woman every night. Me, I want a workshop. Paul, he wants a friend. Irishman, he wants a bed, and Hans, he just want the million dollars. Big opportunity! Come on, Peter, a big dream.

PETER [*looking around*]: All this gone?

DIMITRI: You said so. One morning you come here, to this street here, and the kitchen is gone. And you look around for more kitchens and is none anywhere. What you want to do? The United Nations wants to know.

[PETER, *suddenly confronted with his own idea, becomes embarrassed and shy. He laughs his silly laugh.* 'Hya, hya, hya, hya.' *Kicks the cardboard box.* 'Hya, hya, hya.' *And then* MONIQUE *arrives, bringing in the last dishes, and* PETER *forgets everything and becomes the all-consumed lover, the excited child.*]

MONIQUE: Ready?

PETER: Finished? I come, I come. Hey, Irishman, you'll soon be coming back. Go home. Change. You catch pneumonia. [*Excitedly.*] *Auf geht's, auf geht's!*

[*The mad* PETER *rushes out with his* MONIQUE.
The rest are left.
The guitar and the hum of the ovens.]

DIMITRI [*shouting at the absent Peter*]: Fool! Bloody fool! We wait for a dream.

PAUL: I don't know what you see in him.

DIMITRI: I don't know what I see in him either. Bloody fool!

KEVIN: Bloody volcano, if you ask me. I'm away. [*Rises.*]

PAUL [*returning to his work*]: He hasn't got a dream.

KEVIN: It's all mad talk if you ask me. I don't see no point in it. I don't see no point in that Peter bloke either. He talks about peace and dreams and when I ask him if I could use his cutting board to cut me lemons on this morning he told me – get your own. Dreams! See yous!

[KEVIN *exits.*
HANS *is still playing.*]

DIMITRI *returns to his sweeping.*]

PAUL [*to Dimitri*]: So *you* tell me that point of all that. I don't even know what I was saying myself.

DIMITRI: Why should I know? Sometimes things happen and no one sees the point – and then suddenly, something else happen and you see the point. Peter not a fool! You not a fool! People's brain moves all the time. *All* the time. I'm telling you.

[DIMITRI *sweeps on.*

HANS *continues singing.*

The LIGHTS *slowly fade.*]

ACT TWO

[*Everyone has returned for the evening work. The waitresses have been served with their food, the cooks have settled down some five minutes ago to their own meal. As the curtain rises* PAUL *and* RAYMOND *are in the last stages of their day's work.* MICHAEL, KEVIN, GASTON, *and* HANS *are at the table near the pastrycooks.* ALFREDO *and* PETER *are eating at Alfredo's usual spot.* FRANK, MAX, *and* NICHOLAS *are seated as in the morning. The* CHEF *is by his table writing. Some of the porters are leaning by the walls talking, one or two waitresses wander in or out. The coffee woman is eating with* BERTHA. PETER *is lying with his head in his arms.*]

ALFREDO [*to Peter*]: You are not ill, are you?

PETER [*his head all the time in his arms*]: No.

ALFREDO: Good! You have all your teeth?

PETER: Yes.

ALFREDO: Good! You have good lodgings?

PETER: Yes.

ALFREDO: You eat enough, don't you?

PETER: Yes.

ALFREDO: So tell me what you're unhappy for.

PETER [*raising his head*]: Alfredo, you are a good cook, uh? You come in the morning, you go straight to work, you ask nobody anything, you tell nobody anything. You are ready to start work before we are, you never panic. Tell me, is this a good house?

ALFREDO [*dryly*]: Depends. It's not bad for Mr Marango, you know.

MICHAEL [*approaching Peter*]: Peter, give me a cigarette, please! [PETER *does so*, MICHAEL *stays on to listen.*]

ALFREDO: I'm an old man. It's finished for me. Mind you, I've worked in places where I could do good cooking. But it doesn't matter now. Now I work only for the money.

MICHAEL: Quite right! A match, Peter, please.

PETER [*to Michael, as he looks for matches*]: You like it here, don't you? No, I got no matches.

MICHAEL: The ovens, I love the sound of the ovens.

PETER: Idiot! He loves the sound of the ovens! You stand before them all day! They're red hot! You fry first a bit of ham and an egg in a tin; then someone orders an onion soup and you put soup and bread and cheese in another tin and you grill that. Then someone orders an omelette and you rush to do that. Then someone throws you a hamburger and you fry that. You go up, you go down, you jump here, you jump there; you sweat till steam comes off your back.

MICHAEL [*moving across to Nick for a light*]: I love it.

PETER [*returning head to arms*]: Good luck to you.

MAX [*to Nick*]: What did you marry her for then?

MICHAEL [*holding out his hand to Nick*]: Got a light, Nick?

NICK [*loudly (they are both drunk) as he feels for matches*]: Because I love her, that's why. Ha – [*digs Frank*] – did you hear that? Why did I marry her? Because I love her. And you? [*Hands* MICHAEL *matches.*] Here.

MAX [*enjoying his joke uproariously and also digging Frank*]: Because she told me I was big for my age. [*When his laughter has died down*] Hey, did you read about the man who took a young girl into his house, his wife was there, and they all sat undressed watching television. His wife was there! With him! All undressed! Watching television!

FRANK [*dryly, he too is drunk*]: So what happened? They caught cold? [MICHAEL *wanders back to the third table.*]

KEVIN: I'll be taking *my* leave tonight, by Christ.

GASTON: But you'll get used to it. It's good money.

[*At this point a waitress strolls up to listen.*]

KEVIN: To hell with the money an' all. I like me pay but not for this. It's too big here, man; it's high pressure all the time. An' the food! Look at the food! I never cooked so bad since I was in the army. An' no one is after caring much either!

WAITRESS: And what about the waitresses? We're the animals! Here, you know at the banquet the other day, when we had Minestrone soup . . .

HANS: Huh! Minestrone soup! A drop of meat stock and salt!

WAITRESS: . . . there were about ten of us, some extras as well. Well, the head waiter gave us the signal to get out plates, and oh my God, the mad rush. Everybody pushing everybody else out of the way. Look – [shows arm]. One of the extras did it. It makes you an animal it does; I was telling my . . .

HANS [to Kevin]: Marango will try to make you stay.

KEVIN: Now there's a man. Have you watched him? One of the girls dropped some cups by there this morning and he cried 'Me wages,' he cried. 'All me wages down there!' And do you take notice of the way he strolls among us all? I thought he'd a kind face but when he's done talking with you his kindliness evaporates. In thin air it goes, sudden, and his face gets worried as though today were the last day and he had to be a closing for good and he were taking a last sad glance at everything going on. This mornin' he watched me a while and then walked away shaking his head as though I were dying and there was not a drop of hope for me left an' all.

HANS [to Gaston]: What he has said?

[GASTON laughs and digs Kevin. The waitress wanders away, but not before she flirtatiously kisses PAUL who has just strolled up.]

PAUL [to those at the table]: Bon appétit.

GASTON: Paul, you got some cake?

PAUL [to Ray]: Ray, we got any cake? [RAY brings some over.] [To Hans] You got over this morning yet?

HANS [taking one of the cakes RAY is offering round]: This morning, ach! He's a big fool that Max. He's like a dustbin.

RAY: So why you take notice? Look at them.

[FRANK is still eating, MAX and NICHOLAS are standing up and pointing at each other in some sort of argument, waving fingers, pulling faces, and swaying.]

RAY: The first thing in the morning they come in and drink a bottle of beer. Then they're happy. All day they drink. [*Returns to work.*]

PAUL [*to Hans*]: What did Max say then, exactly?

HANS: He doesn't like I talk in German. [*Tragically.*] You know, Paul, you – you are a Jew and me – I'm a German; we suffer together. [*Nods his head to emphasize the sad situation.*] We suffer together.

[*PAUL laughs ironically, slaps Hans on the back, and returns to his work.*]

KEVIN: Is that a Jew then?

HANS [*sentimentally*]: A very good boy.

KEVIN: Well, who'd have thought that now!

[*At this point a TRAMP wanders into the kitchen. He is looking for the CHEF. Everyone stares at him and grins.*]

MAX [*shouting across to Bertha*]: Bertha, ha, ha, is this your old man come after you? [*General laughter.*]

[*The TRAMP comes over to the group of young men and talks to Kevin.*]

TRAMP: 'Scuse me. The Chef please, which'n is he?

[*The CHEF wanders slowly up to the man, trying to assume an intimidating expression. He says nothing but merely raises his head questioningly.*]

TRAMP: 'Scuse me, Chef. [*Touching his knee.*] War disabled. I don't usually ask for food, but I lost me pensions book, see? I don't like to ask but . . .

[*The CHEF turns to Michael and points to the soup. At the same time he says to a porter, 'Clean a tin,' and then he returns to his place.*]

TRAMP [*to Kevin*]: Don't usually do this. Can't do anything till they trace me book. [*To Hans*] Got it in the desert, 'gainst Rommel.

[*HANS looks away. After an embarrassing few seconds' silence MICHAEL returns with a fruit tin full of soup and hands it to the tramp.*]

TRAMP [*realizing he hasn't received much, tries again*]: Got a cigarette?

MAX: Go on, 'op it, be quick, we got work.

PETER [*goes up to tramp and looks in the tin. He takes tin from tramp and offers it to Max*]: You drink it?

MAX: Ah, get out of it, you and your high and bloody mighty gestures. *I* work for my living. Fool!

[PETER *ignores him and tosses the tin into the dustbin. Then he moves to Hans' station and brings back two meat cutlets which he gives to the tramp.*]

PETER: Take these cutlets. [*Gently pushing him.*] Now go, quick, whist!

[*But he is not quick enough. The* CHEF *approaches and stands looking on.*]

CHEF [*quietly*]: What's that?

PETER: I gave him some cutlets.

CHEF [*still quietly*]: Mr Marango told you to give him?

PETER: No, but . . .

CHEF: You heard me say perhaps?

PETER: No, I . . .

CHEF: You have authority suddenly?

PETER [*impatiently*]: So what's a couple of cutlets, we going bankrupt or something?

CHEF: It's four and six, that's what, and it's me who's Chef that's what and – [PETER *moves away muttering* 'Ach'. *The* CHEF *follows him, annoyed now.*] Don't think we're too busy I can't sack you. Three years is nothing you know; you don't buy the place in three years, you hear me? You got that? Don't go thinking I won't sack you.

[*By this time* MR MARANGO *appears on his round, hands in pocket.* TRAMP *finds this an opportunity to go. With a gesture of the head* MARANGO *asks what is the matter.* CHEF *does not wish to make any more fuss.*]

CHEF: The tramp, Peter gave him a cutlet, it was his own supper.

[CHEF *returns to his work, dispersing the crowd on the way.* MR MARANGO *simply nods his head at Peter. It is a sad nodding, as*

though Peter had just insulted him. He walks from right of stage
to the left in a half circle round Peter nodding his head all the
time.]

MARANGO [softly]: Sabotage. [Pause.] It's sabotage you do to me.
[Sadly taking his right hand out of his pocket and waving it round the
kitchen.] It's my fortune here and you give it away. [He moves off
muttering 'Sabotage'.]

PETER: But it . . .

MARANGO [not even bothering to look round]: Yes, yes, I'm always
wrong – of course – yes, yes. [Moves off into dining room.]
[Everyone settles back into place. PETER goes to get a cup of coffee and
makes faces at Marango's back; then he returns beside Alfredo. HANS
joins them.]

HANS: Er ist wirklich hinter dir, her?

PETER: Ach, er erwartet, dass die ganze Welt auf seine Küche aufpasst.]

KEVIN: I seem to remember being told not to grumble by someone.

PETER: A bastard man. A bastard house.

KEVIN: And he also said you could get used to anything.

PETER: But this house is like – is like –

PAUL: Yeah? What is it like?

PETER: God in heaven, I don't know what it's like. If only it – if
only it –

KEVIN: Yes, yes, we know all that – if only it would all go.

PETER: Just one morning – to find it gone.

PAUL: Fat lot of good you'd be if it went – you couldn't even cough
up a dream when it was necessary.

PETER: A dream?

HANS: Yes, mein Lieber – the dream, remember? You walked out on
us.

PETER: A dream! [Thinks about it sadly.] I can't dream in a kitchen.
[As if to prove the point the work in the kitchen is heard extra loud.
MONIQUE comes front of stage and leans on centre of counter with a
cup of coffee. PETER goes up to her. MICHAEL and HANS wander
back to their table.]

MONIQUE [*with great sentimentality*]: Did you see that tramp? Isn't that a shame?

PETER: You didn't hear?

MONIQUE: Hear what?

PETER [*boasting and laughing*]: I had a row about him. Mr Marango and the Chef there. They wanted to give him a dirty tin full of soup so I threw it away and gave him some cutlets.

MONIQUE: Oh you didn't, Peter. . . . And Marango caught you?

PETER [*imitating*]: 'Sabotage,' the old man said. 'Sabotage, all my fortune you take away.'

MONIQUE [*pushing him playfully with her hand*]: Oh, Peter!

PETER [*tenderly*]: I brought your birthday present.

MONIQUE [*placing her arm round his neck joyfully*]: Tell me, tell me, what is it, ah? What is it?

PETER [*taking her in his arms*]: You wait, yes?

[MONIQUE *embraces him and her hand slips to his buttocks which she nips. They playfully struggle for a few seconds in which time another waitress passes them and takes Monique's hand off Peter's behind and places it on his shoulders, crying, 'Now then, Monique, watch it!'*]

MONIQUE [*coyly replacing her hand*]: But it's nice.

PETER: Can you eat me?

MONIQUE: Oh, don't be silly, Peter.

PETER: How do you want me? Grilled? Fried? Underdone? Well done?

[*While* PETER *and* MONIQUE *continue to talk affectionately a sudden cry comes up from the back of the kitchen. That waitress who has just passed Peter and Monique has doubled up in pain and passed out. A crowd rushes to her – it all happens very quickly, hardly noticed. The boys at the table simply glance round and watch but do not move.* PETER *and* MONIQUE *do not even hear it. We can only hear a few confused voices.*]

FIRST VOICE: What's happened?

SECOND VOICE: Winnie has passed out.

THIRD VOICE: All right, now, don't crowd round, take her into the dining room. Don't crowd round. [*Crowd disperses as* WINNIE *is taken into dining room.*]

KEVIN: Well, what was all that now?

GASTON: The heat. Always affecting someone. Terrible.

    [*Meanwhile . . .*]

PETER [*to Monique*]: Did you – er – you still going to do it? I mean I . . .

MONIQUE: Don't worry, Peter, I shall see to it now. It's not the first time, is it?

PETER: You don't think we should go through with it? I don't mind being responsible, you know that.

MONIQUE: Enough, I'm not going to talk about it any more.

PETER: You told Monty about us, then?

MONIQUE [*finishing her coffee*]: You really must stop rowing with Marango, darling.

PETER: Did you speak to Monty as we said?

MONIQUE: They won't stand it all the time, you know. I'm always telling you about this, Peter.

PETER: Listen, Monique, I love you. Please listen to me that I love you. You said you love me but you don't say to your husband this thing.

MONIQUE: Now not this again.

PETER: You are not going to leave him, are you? You don't really intend it?

MONIQUE: Oh, Peter, please.

PETER: What do you want I should do then?

MONIQUE: Did the Chef say much?

PETER: We could leave any day. We could go for a long holiday first. Skiing in Switzerland perhaps.

MONIQUE: I am going to the hairdresser tomorrow as well.

PETER: Monique, we row this morning, we row in the afternoon too, this evening we are almost in love again. Answer me.

MONIQUE: Monty has promised we shall soon have our own house.

PETER [*screaming*]: MONIQUE!

[MONIQUE *looks round in embarrassment and, muttering 'You fool', stalks off. A waitress approaches Peter.*]

WAITRESS: You serving yet, Peter? I want three turbot. Special for Marango.

PETER: It's half-past six yet?

WAITRESS: It's nearly . . .

PETER: Half-past six is service.

WAITRESS: But it's special . . .

PETER: HALF-PAST SIX!

[PETER *goes off to find some beer. Service is just beginning. Evening service is not so hectic and takes a longer time to start up. Waitresses appear, most people are at their stations, the people at the table near the pastry section are just rising.*]

KEVIN: Me, I'd have a Jaguar. It's got a luxury I could live with.

GASTON: Have you seen the new French Citröen? Just like a mechanical frog it looks.

HANS: And the Volkswagen? It's not a good car?

KEVIN: Now there's a good little car for little money.

HANS: No country makes like the Volkswagen.

KEVIN: You've gotta hand it to the German.

[PETER *has returned with a bottle of beer. He cries out his laughter and sings his song. More waitresses are coming in but the service is easy and orders ring out in comfort. One waitress, however, breaks her journey round the kitchen and, wiping some plates which she has just taken from the hot plate, goes up to the* CHEF *to gossip.* MAX *and* NICHOLAS *stand by listening.*]

WAITRESS: Heard what happened to Winnie? She's been rushed to hospital.

MAX: What did she do wrong then?

WAITRESS: She was pregnant.

MAX: She didn't look it.

WAITRESS: I know. She didn't give herself a chance.

CHEF: Misfired?

WAITRESS: I'll say, and it weren't no accident neither.

MAX [*shaking his head*]: Silly woman, silly woman.

CHEF: She's got seven children already, though.

WAITRESS: That's right. Marango's hopping mad. It started happening on the spot, in there, in the dining room. May and Sophie had to take her away.

MAX: What did she do then?

WAITRESS: She took pills, that's what. And I'll tell you something else, there are four other girls here took the same pills. There! Four of them! And you know who one of the four is? [*She inclines her head in Peter's direction.*]

MAX: Monique?

WAITRESS [*nodding her head triumphantly*]: Now don't you tell anyone I told you, mind. But you ask Hettie, ask her, she bought the stuff. [*Continues on the round.*]

MAX: Knew this would happen. Knew it! Can't be done though. What makes them think that by taking a tablet through the mouth it'll affect the womb? There is only one way, the way it went in! What happens with a tablet? Nothing! Nothing can. The stomach is irritated that's all, squeezed, see? Forces the womb, presses it.

NICK: Now what do you know about this? A doctor now!

MAX: Oh, I know about this all right. Only one drug is effective through the mouth. [*Secretively.*] And you know what that is? Ergot? Heard of it? Only thing to do it. And that's rare. Oh yes, I studied this in the forces when I had nothing else to do. Very interesting, this psychology. Complicated. I knew Winnie was pregnant soon as she came here.

[*All this time the pastrycooks have been clearing away their station and are now ready to go. They are saying good-bye to everyone.* MAX *shouts to them as they go.*]

MAX: Some people have it easy!

[*The pastrycooks leave and as they do so an argument flares up*

139

suddenly at Peter's station, PETER *takes a silver plate with fish in it out of a waitress's hand and smashes it to the floor. She had just helped herself to her order while* PETER *had been busy and his back turned.*]

PETER: You wait for me, yes? *I* serve you. You ask *me.*

WAITRESS: But you were busy.

PETER: I don't care. This is my place and there [*points to the side of bar*], there is for you.

WAITRESS: Now you wait a bloody minute, will you? Who the hell do you think you are, you?

PETER: You don't worry who I am. I'm a cook, yes? And you're the waitress, and in the kitchen you do what I like, yes? And in the dining room you do what you like.

WAITRESS [*taking another plate from the oven*]: I won't take orders from you you know, I . . .

PETER [*shouting and smashing the plate from her hand for a second time*]: Leave it! Leave it there! I'll serve you. Me! Me! Is *my* kingdom here. This is the side where *I* live. *This.*

WAITRESS: You Bosch you. You bloody German bastard!

[*She downs plates on the bar and walks off.* PETER *follows her. There is a general uproar and protest from the other waitresses who are impatient to be served.*]

PETER: What you call me? What was it? Say it again. [*But she has gone right off into the dining room. He screams at her.*] SAY IT AGAIN!

[*This scream calls the attention of most people to him. They all stare at him as at a frightened animal.* PETER *stands aroused, left back of stage, with his back to the audience. Suddenly he wheels round and in a frenzy searches for something violent to do. First he darts forward, then stops; then he rushes to his right and stops again. Then with a cry of 'Auf geht's' he dashes to a part under the serving counter near Michael and picking up a chopper from the bar smashes something underneath. There is a slow hiss and all the fires of the oven die down. There is a second of complete silence before anybody realizes what has happened, and then* FRANK *and two others are upon him, trying to hold him down. The* CHEF, *at last moved to do something, rushes to the scene, but* PETER *breaks away and flees to the dining room.* FRANK *and others follow. All this happened too quickly for anyone to do a great deal about it, but in the scuffle the following cries are heard:*]

MICHAEL: He's broken the gas lead! Someone turn off the main!

FRANK: Hold him, grab hold of him!

KEVIN: Jesus Christ, he'll murder her.

HANS: *Sei nicht dumm! Beherrsch dich! Lass' ihn laufen!*

[*When* PETER *has rushed into the dining room there is another silence as everybody waits to hear what will happen next. Some are not even sure what has already happened. A crowd has gathered by the glass partition through which can be seen the dining room. Suddenly there is a tremendous crash of crockery to the ground. Some waitresses and, presumably, customers scream.*]

KEVIN: Holy Mother o' Mary, he's gone berserk.

GASTON: The lunatic! He's swept all the plates off the table in there.

MICHAEL [*who is one of the crowd by the glass partition, moves away down to the front of stage*]: He's ripped his hands.

KEVIN: I knew something like this would happen, now I just knew it. When you take away a man's dignity he is fighting mad. Can you see that now? Can you understand it now?

[*The crowd by the entrance to the dining room make way as* FRANK, ALFREDO, *and* HANS *bring* PETER *back. Peter's hands are covered in blood. Some smears have reached his face. He looks terribly exhausted. They bring him down stage.* MICHAEL *hurriedly finds a stool.*]

CHEF [*to Michael*]: Phone an ambulance.

WAITRESS: Monique is doing that now.

[MONIQUE *pushes through the crowd. She is sobbing, but she carries the medical box and a table-cloth.* ALFREDO *snatches the cloth from her and rips it up. She tries to dab some liquid on Peter's hands; he*

jumps. This is too much for her: she leaves it all and rushes away.
ALFREDO, *however, simply takes Peter's hands and ties them up.*]

PETER: It hurts, Christ, it hurts.

ALFREDO: Shut up!

CHEF [*bending close to Peter*]: Fool! [*He straightens up and finding nothing else to say for the moment bends down to repeat again:*] Fool! [*Pause.*] So? What? The whole kitchen is stopped. Fool!

PETER [*to Alfredo*]: Now he cares.

CHEF [*incredulous and furious*]: What do you mean, 'Now he cares'?

ALFREDO [*gently moving* CHEF *out of the way that he might tie up Peter's hands*]: Leave him, Chef, leave him now.

CHEF [*reaching Peter another way*]: What do you mean, 'Now he cares'? *You* have to make me care? Forty years and suddenly you have to make me care? You? You? Who are you, tell me? In all this big world who are you, for Christ's sake?

[*At this point the crowd breaks away to let* MARANGO *in. He looks like a man who has just lost all his money at the stock exchange, as though he might have a fit. At first he is unable to speak. All he does is gesticulate with his arms in the air showing Peter what he has done* –]

MARANGO: You have stopped my whole world. [*Pause.*] Did you get permission from God? Did you? [*He looks to the others – perhaps they heard God give Peter permission. Then to Peter.*] There-is-no-one-else! You know that? NO ONE!

FRANK [*taking Marango's shoulder*]: All right, take it easy, Marango. The boy is going, he's going. He's ill, don't upset yourself.

MARANGO [*turning to Frank and making a gentle appeal*]: Why does everybody sabotage me, Frank? I give work, I pay well, yes? They eat what they want, don't they? I don't know what more to give a man. He works, he eats, I give him money. This is life, isn't it? I haven't made a mistake, have I? I live in the right world, don't I? [*To Peter*] And you've stopped this world. A shnip! A boy! You've stopped it. Well why? Maybe you can tell me something I don't know – just tell me. [*No answer.*] I want to learn something. [*To Frank*] Is there something I don't know? [PETER *rises and in pain moves off. When he reaches a point back centre stage* MARANGO *cries at him:*] BLOODY FOOL! [*Rushes round to him.*] What more do you want? What is there more, tell me? [*He shakes Peter but gets no reply.* PETER *again tries to leave. Again* MARANGO *cries out:*] What is there more? [PETER *stops, turns in pain and sadness, shakes his head as if to say – if you don't know I cannot explain. And so he moves right off stage.* MARANGO *is left facing his staff who stand around, almost accusingly, looking at him. And he asks again –*] What is there more? What *is* there more?

[*We have seen that there must be something more and so the* LIGHTS *must slowly fade.*]

CURTAIN

BERNARD KOPS

The Hamlet of Stepney Green

A SAD COMEDY
WITH SOME SONGS

THE HAMLET OF STEPNEY GREEN

First presented by the Meadow Players Limited at the Playhouse, Oxford, on 19 May 1958, with the following cast:

THE CHILDREN	Marie Seaborne
	Linda Blackledge
	Janet Derry
HAVA SEGAL	Ruth Meyers
MR SEGAL	John Barrard
SAM LEVY	Harold Lang
DAVID LEVY	John Fraser
BESSIE LEVY	Dorothea Phillips
MR STONE	Joss Ackland
MRS STONE	Pat Keen
MR GREEN	Gilbert Vernon
MR BLACK	Christopher Hancock
MR WHITE	Robert Bernal
ACCORDIONIST	Leon Rosselson

Directed by Frank Hauser

The play was transferred to the Lyric Opera House, Hammersmith, on 15 July 1958. In this production the part of BESSIE LEVY was played by Thelma Ruby.

CHARACTERS OF THE PLAY

SAM LEVY: 65, *small and agile, a pickled-herring seller of Wentworth Street*
BESSIE LEVY: 52, *attractive, his wife. Plump and wears cheap jewellery*
DAVID LEVY: 22, *their son; tall and intelligent. Wants to be a crooner*
SOLLY SEGAL: 60, *retired. A friend of the family*
HAVA SEGAL: 18, *beautiful, and sure of herself. Has just returned from Israel*
MR STONE: *Fat and jovial; foolish and about fifty years old*
MRS STONE: *Fat and foolish; jovial and about fifty years old*
MR WHITE: *About 32, looks older. Insurance agent, over-positive and smug*
MR BLACK: 27, *well dressed. A tombstone salesman. Small and thin*
MR GREEN: 27, *well dressed. A tombstone salesman. Small and fat*
THREE CHILDREN: *Sing and dance*

ACT ONE

The action of the play is centred around the house of MR *and* MRS LEVY
Time: *The present.*
Place: *Stepney Green in the East End of London.*

*The setting is constant throughout and the stage is in two sections; one half
is part of the house, showing a cross section of the living-room and the
corridor. The living-room has the various pieces of furniture that one would
expect in a Jewish lower middle-class family, not too much bad taste is
apparent; the furnishing should be sparse and straightforward.*
The other half should be the garden of the LEVYS. *There are flowers in rich
profusion but this garden is surrounded by a great area of bomb damage;
it gives the hint of almost being an oasis; there is a fence around the garden,
and a gate leading off* L: *there should be a certain warmth about the set, as if
Van Gogh and Chagall had collaborated on this urban scene.*

[*Curtain goes up revealing an empty stage. It is a very hot July
afternoon; nearby some* CHILDREN *are heard skipping and singing:*]

CHILDREN [*off*]: On the hill there stands a lady, who she is I do not
know; all she wants is gold and silver, all she wants is a fine young
man.

[*A ball comes over the fence and the* CHILDREN *run on stage after it;
they explore the garden and sniff the flowers and then they begin to
sing again.*]

On the hill there stands a lady, who she is I do not know –

[*They are dancing round in a ring when they are interrupted by* HAVA
who comes into the garden from the house.]

HAVA: Here, go on and buy some ice-cream; play in the park. [*She
hands one of the children a sixpence; they just stare at her.*] Please run
away and play; Mr Levy isn't feeling too well.

[*The* CHILDREN *run off and sing as they exit.*]

CHILDREN: All she wants is gold and silver, all she wants is a fine young man.

[*They exit.*]

HAVA: Don't we all. [*She sits down and reads a woman's magazine.*]

BESSIE [*off*]: I said no! ... N ... O ... NO, no, no, NO.

SAM [*off*]: I tell you yes: YE-YES. All my life I worked in the open air and you bet your life, I'm going to die there ... Come on, Mr Segal, push me into the garden.

BESSIE [*off*]: All right, I should worry! It's your funeral!

SAM [*off*]: You said it.

[*A small man is seen trying to push a bed into the garden from the back room; HAVA immediately gets up and helps MR SEGAL, her father, and both of them manage to push the bed into the centre of the garden; MR SEGAL is immaculately dressed and smokes a cigar.*]

MR SEGAL: Is this spot all right? Just here, Sam?

[*A frail old man levers himself up from his lying position in the bed; it is SAM and he wears pyjamas; he looks around.*]

SAM: This'll do fine. Just here. Thank you, Mr Segal. What a lovely day! What a lovely daughter you have! She's a credit to you; what's the matter, Hava? Why did you come back home? Didn't you like it out in Israel?

HAVA: It wasn't bad, but I was lonely; the life was different out there. I couldn't seem to settle down. England's where I belong. At least I've learned that much.

SAM: Still, you're looking very well. I was telling my Davey to go there; he wouldn't listen.

HAVA: I am looking forward to meeting your son David again. How is he, Mr Levy?

MR SEGAL: A lot of good that boy will be to you, anywhere in the world. Excuse me, Sam, but you must agree; he's good for nothing.

SAM: There I disagree with you, Mr Segal, he'll find his feet; he's going through a difficult phase, he's not so bad.

MR SEGAL: He's been going through this difficult phase for fifteen years; it's about time he settled down; it's your fault, you're not strict enough.

HAVA: I think David is a lovely boy; he's got such a wonderful voice, he'll go a long way.

MR SEGAL: The longer the way, the better. What a voice! Sam, she drives me mad talking about him. It wouldn't have been such a bad idea for your son and my daughter to – well – if he had a nice job with prospects, but a crooner? Hava, you've got a screw loose.

SAM: Hava, do you like my boy? Do you? Maybe you can help him. Help him to see sense; persuade him to give up his crazy ideas; does he like you?

HAVA: Like me? He never even sees me. He looks straight through me. The other day I passed him by near Brick Lane; he was just staring at the sky: I said 'Hello, Davey.' He didn't even bother to look my way! Oh well, what can you do?

SAM: It isn't natural. He's ambitious. I said: 'Look, Davey, all right I'll help you; go and study music, learn all about notes,' but he refused.

HAVA: He's got a wonderful voice. He was always such a gentle boy.

SAM: If that is a wonderful voice then I'm Gregory Peck.

HAVA: He's got a lovely voice. He'll go a long way. You'll see.

SAM: What did you miss out there?

HAVA: I missed the cinemas and the dance halls; all my friends. I missed my own room and my own bed. I was homesick.

SAM: Are you going back?

HAVA: No. I don't think so; it's unwise to go back. I'm not fooling myself. I'm no pioneer.

SAM: I suppose you're right; anyway, everything turns out for the best. You'll meet a nice respectable boy, you'll settle down, get a nice flat and you'll get everything you want and deserve. You're attractive, you'll have no trouble.

HAVA: I hope so. Where's Davey now?

SAM: How should I know? Who knows where that boy is, even when he's here?

MR SEGAL: Forget about him! Do you know, Sam, she drives me mad, all day she's talking about him! What's he got, I wonder? What's he got that others ain't?

SAM: By the way it sounds, it seems he has a wonderful voice. What can you do with them?

HAVA: Here you go again! The younger generation! Good-bye, Daddy. [*She kisses Mr Segal.*] I promised Miriam that I'd go over this afternoon. Don't come home too late. Good-bye, Mr Levy, take care of yourself. [*They shake hands.*] Good-bye. [*She exits.*]

SAM: What a nice girl! Do you know, Mr Segal, that for many years I thought about today. I wondered what it would be like when I died; I wondered what the weather would be like and if I would be nervous. It's funny, for years I've worried that I wouldn't have the chance to die naturally. I thought that it would be the A-Bomb or the H-Bomb or the Z-Bomb or bacteria, rockets, or gas, yet here I am on a fine summer's day going to die quietly in my garden; why, I never even retired, never even moved to Golders Green.

MR SEGAL: I know what you mean. Mr Miller was killed the other day by a van; he was worried about the world situation and was reading a newspaper as he crossed the road; you remember Mr Miller?

SAM: Not off-hand.

[*The* CHILDREN *have returned to the outside of the garden again; once more they start singing.*]

CHILDREN [*singing off*]: Julius Caesar, such a silly geezer, caught his head in a lemon squeezer.

MR SEGAL: I'll go and stop that noise; they should be ashamed of themselves. I tell you, Sam, the children of today –

[*He is about to go when* SAM *catches hold of his sleeve.*]

SAM: No, no, Mr Segal, let them sing; let them sing. Let everybody sing. Music makes the world go round. Mr Segal, you should never stop a child from singing. You should be ashamed of yourself, a man of your age. Tomorrow I'd give my right arm for the slightest sound from the tiniest throat.

MR SEGAL: What do you mean, Sam? You talk in riddles.

SAM: I mean that I shan't be here tomorrow. I won't have a right arm to give away. [*He is looking at his right arm and is shaking it.*] It's all over, Mr Segal. Life slipped through my fingers and as it was slipping, that was life.

MR SEGAL: Of course. What do you mean?

SAM: I mean, life was no other time, no other place; it is here and now and gone. I came in at Odessa sixty-five years ago and today I'm going to die in Stepney Green, that's what I mean.

MR SEGAL: Don't be silly, Sam. You're not going to die, you're a bit delirious. If I died every time I thought like that I would have had forty or fifty coffins. Don't talk silly, you make me feel miserable.

SAM: I'm sorry. No, this is it, believe me. I've got more than a cold, I can tell you. I've been frightened recently; I've lain awake nearly all night and broke out into a terrible cold sweat when I realized that I was getting older and older and that I was getting nearer and nearer – to nothing! You can't run away from death, Mr Segal, there's no escaping it, it catches you in the end; my end is here and now, and now I'm resigned to it.

MR SEGAL: You've got a very vivid imagination, Sam; that's always been your trouble; now I know who your David takes after.

SAM: He takes after my grandfather's brother, according to what I heard about him, Manny Levy, got in with a bad crowd; but with a heart of gold. He ran away with an actress and everyone talked about it. [*Pause*] Mr Segal, now I realize that I never lived; all my life I've been asleep. Been dead! My physical death will prove for ever that there was never anyone called Samuel Levy, pickled-herring seller of Wentworth Street; two children and a widow; you'll read all about it in the *Jewish Chronicle* next week; they'll make up a little rhyme and then someone will come and sell my wife a stone.

MR SEGAL: Sam, what's come over you? You make me sad talking like this.

SAM: Don't upset yourself on my account. It hasn't been a bad life. Have the boys missed me in the market? Have any of them asked after me?

MR SEGAL: Yes. Moishe Newman told me to remind you that you still owe him thirty shillings.

SAM: Yes, I remember, for the chickens; tell Bessie, would you? She'll take care of everything. Thank God I've got myself insured, tomorrow she's got two hundred and fifty pounds coming to her.

MR SEGAL: Such money she can do without. What is going to matter if you die, anyway? Don't make me laugh; you're not going to die.

SAM: We're all going to die; you don't have to be a prophet to know that. I'm worried about my herring stall. I shall have to talk to Davey and make him see sense; he's got to get rid of these bright ideas; he's no longer a kid.

MR SEGAL: Why don't you try to rest now, Sam? Try and sleep.

SAM [*he sits right up in bed and leans forward*]: Try to sleep? Rest? Do me a favour. I've got a lot of rest coming to me, I can tell you. No – I must keep awake and take everything in; I want to be more observant today than I have ever been. Smoking cigars, eh. You bloody miser, how can you afford them on the old age pension? I always suspected that you had a tidy sum stuck away. Come on, own up, I'm a dying man.

MR SEGAL: My boy sends them to me from New York; he sends me fifty dollars a month, also; he's a good boy. I spoke to him on the telephone two months ago. He's got a proper Yank accent. He's married there to a girl.

SAM: I didn't think that he married a boy; what does he do for a living?

MR SEGAL: He travels; business, you know.

[SAM *nods*.]

I tell you, my children are as good as gold. Hava even came back to look after me when her mother died; she's just like a little mother, what would I have done without them?

SAM: Children, oy vay, don't talk to me about children. All your life you sweat your kishkers out to give them a good education and everything they want and what happens? Davey turns around and tells me that two and two don't add up to four, and Lottie joins the Communist Party. The Communist Party I can stand, but to add insult to injury she runs away with a goy; I've pushed it all inside me and I've swallowed it, so please don't talk about children.

MR SEGAL: Still, David isn't as bad as all that.

SAM: He was all right until he started going up west when he was 17; soon as his pimples went so do he, drifting from job to job, more out than in, getting a craze over one thing after another; but for years now he's been crooning and when he's not crooning he's listening to records of crooners; I wish he'd even go out sometimes but now he's got a new habit. He sits in the house every evening, mooching around and sighing. Who knows where it will end? Come on, give us a cigar, you stingy old sod.

[SAM *gets out of bed, to* MR SEGAL'S *horror. He walks over to* MR SEGAL *and* MR SEGAL *gravely hands him a cigar and lights it for him.* SAM *paces around the stage puffing at the cigar.* DAVID *comes on. He hovers in background. He is dressed in a well-made suit.*]

SAM: Beggars can't be choosers,
　　So pass the word around,
　　No matter what you do,
　　You'll end up underground.

[MR SEGAL *tries to steer him back to bed but* SAM *refuses to go and walks around the stage looking at imaginary fruit and groceries.* DAVID *follows them, unseen. He sings.*]

DAVID [*sings*]: Silver trout are sleeping in heaps upon the slabs,
　　　　　　With mackerel and lobsters and lethargic crabs.
　　　　　　The dead are busy sleeping eternity away,
　　　　　　They cannot go out shopping on this fair summer's
　　　　　　　day.

SEGAL
SAM: } [*sing*]: Beggars can't be choosers, the executioner said,
And if you beg for life, you're bound to lose your head.

DAVID [*sings*]: They do not smell the flowers that take the breath away

Mimosa and Rose, Carnation and Lily;

The dead are busy sleeping in the eternal dark,

They do not go out shopping or walk in the park.

SEGAL
SAM: } [*sing*]: Beggars can't be choosers, so pass the world away,
No matter how you climb, you'll end up in the clay.

DAVID [*sings*]: They do not buy the warm bread, the wine and watercress,

Or give a copper coin to a bronze accordionist.

The dead are busy sleeping eternity away,

They come not to the market, on this fair summer's day.

SEGAL
SAM: } [*sing*]: Beggars can't be choosers, no matter what you're worth,

The best of us, the worst of us,

Will burst beneath the earth.

[*They are both standing now arm in arm, breathless and happy.*
DAVID *retires to the background.*]

SAM: Yes, Mr Segal, in the market now there is a glut of cherries, big, ripe, and red, red-currants and black-currants and golden goosegogs as large as Chinese lanterns; grapes, figs, olives, dates, melons, lemons. I tell you, Mr Segal, that's what I've missed.

MR SEGAL: What? Fruit?

SAM [*in the course of this speech music is playing.* SAM *almost breaks out into song but never quite makes it. He speaks slowly*]: Oh, don't be such a bloody fool, of course not. I mean going places and seeing people. After all, that is all that there is in life, going places and seeing people, different places, different people. I promised myself a world trip before I died, to see for myself how people in other countries lived. It never transpired. Working in the market makes

you curious; it does that for you . . . You see the coloured labels
stuck upon the boxes, and you think of the man who packed those
boxes, and of the girl who stuck that label on. You think of the sun
beating down on the wharves and the boat being loaded by sweating men, gently swaying in the golden waves; but – it's too late for
the holiday you planned and you never left the market where you
stand.

MR SEGAL: A vivid imagination, Sam, that's your trouble.

SAM: Beggars can't be choosers, Mr Segal, and my only regret is not
travelling, not having seen California and the Caucasus, Haifa and
Helsinki. I never even saw Odessa again; not that I ever saw it
really. I came on an onion boat to Tilbury when I was 14. Boxes
and boxes of onions on that boat, all with labels stuck on saying
ONIONS, MADE IN RUSSIA. I was also made in Russia, so I came
to Tilbury, and then I came here and I have been here ever since.

BOTH [*sing slowly*]: Beggars can't be choosers,
        So pass the word around,
        You do not need a passport when you travel to
          the ground.

[*The mood changes and* SAM *seems very tired again.*]

SAM: Would you please help me back into bed, Mr Segal?

[MR SEGAL *does so and* SAM *settles down.* DAVID *comes forward. He
speaks very slowly as if every word were a jewel to be weighed and
valued.*]

SAM: Where have you been all day, Davey boy?

DAVID: Whitechapel Art Gallery and the Public Library next door,
that is to say if one should call them that. The Art Gallery contained no art and the Public Library contained no public, just one
or two down-and-outs reading the long newspapers in the racks.

[MR SEGAL *whispers to* DAVID.]

MR SEGAL: David, listen to me, try and be a good boy for a change,
your father is dying.

DAVID: So are we all, all the time.

SAM: Stop whispering, Mr Segal. It's not good manners.

DAVID: Anyway, he looks perfectly all right to me.

SAM: Mr Segal, do me a favour, leave me here with my boy for a moment; I want to talk to him.

[MR SEGAL *is looking over the wall and is shouting at the children who have been making a little noise.*]

MR SEGAL: Go on – do us a favour – play somewhere else, little ruffians. [*He goes off in their direction.*]

CHILDREN [*off*]: Silly Solly Segal – nose like an eagle – eyes like two jelly-fish – teeth like a weasel . . . [*Their voices disappear in the distance.*]

[DAVID *walks round the stage: he stretches his arms exuberantly but he is nervous.*]

SAM: Na Davey, what can I say to you? All these years I wanted you to work in the market with me, then I told myself – 'Don't worry, Sam, he's looking for something better' – well – what are you going to do? No more pie in the sky. You've got to support your mother now.

DAVID: Oh, what can I do?

SAM: You'll have to work.

DAVID: Why should I work when I've got my health and strength? The thought of having to spend the rest of my life looking at the heads of herrings and the heads of hungry people makes me sick.

SAM: What do you think crooners see? Stop dreaming and settle down.

DAVID [*swings around the stage*]: I want to be a crooner – I want to be a king – to be looked at – to be looked up to. I want people to nudge each other as they pass and say 'Look! there goes David Levy – the most famous – fabulous crooner in the world.' I want to hear my voice blaring from the record shops as I whizz by in my Jaguar – I want to switch on the radio – any time – and any day and hear my voice on records.

SAM: Why, Davey? Why have you got these crazy ideas? Who do you take after?

DAVID: I feel good when I'm singing.

SAM: But I'm going to die – who'll look after you?

DAVID: Don't worry about me – I'll be all right, and don't keep on saying you're dying. Whatever happens, though – I won't work down the lane – I refuse – I won't – I'll . . .

SAM: It's not natural – already you're 22 – other boys grow out of these mad ideas already. Other people have only joy from their children – I have a pain in my heart – just my luck. You have no trade – no profession – you're not interested in politics and you drift from job to job – All this has got to stop – I'm a dying man – don't argue.

DAVID: I'm fed up round here. I'm bored. Nothing happens except to other people in the papers. It was bad enough before we got television – now it's worse – everyone sleeps all the time – no one's got any life – now if they gave me a chance on the tele I'd wake them all up – I'd stun them – I'd be the greatest thing – don't ya see – I want to make people happy – I'VE GOT TO MAKE them listen – they'd love me.

SAM: And they call me delirious. What do you want? Look! Tell me – between you and me – I told you the facts of life, didn't I? – Well, you owe me something in exchange – I helped to make you – well, don't make any more nonsense – tell me.

DAVID: You made me all right – you made me what I am. Aren't you proud of me? I know you are deep down – What do you want me to do? – be honest.

SAM: To settle down – take over the business – marry a nice girl.

DAVID: What, and then have a complicated son like me? Something's wrong and you know it. You haven't really been a success because you don't really want me to end up in the market like you – come on, own up.

SAM: Naturally – I expect you to improve – big business man with a wonderful education.

DAVID: You admit, then, you don't want me to have the same life as yourself?

[SAM *cannot reply.*]

It didn't turn out too well, so surely you don't want me to fail – do you? [SAM *cannot reply.*] Well, do you? See – you don't know what to say.

SAM: All I can say is that I don't know where you come from.

DAVID: Singing makes me feel safe – it'll give me a place in the world.

SAM: What a complicated boy I have to turn out!

DAVID: When I croon I feel free.

SAM: Davey – all this nonsense has got to stop.

DAVID: Pipe down – you're dying, remember – we've been through this so many times.

SAM: What a way to treat a father; especially on his death-bed. [*He almost cries.*]

DAVID: Sorry, Dad – but you've been on this death-bed so many times before – don't blackmail me – anyway – why do you want to bequeath me the things you hated – and I know you hated – you told me you hated – as often as you said you were going to kick the bucket – tell me that?

SAM: I shall die a very confused man – now I don't know what I mean.

DAVID: Say that again and anyway even if you were dying how do you do – I'm dying also – dying to be famous and express myself – you'll be all right – It's me I'm worried about – but just give me a chance – Give me time and I'll make you proud of me – So long – I'll be seeing you. I've got some mirror exercises to do. See you soon.

SAM: I wonder.

[DAVID *goes off.* SAM *laughs ironically.* HAVA *enters from the garden and* BESSIE *enters from the house.*]

BESSIE: Sam, Sam. What's the matter with you? Have you been lecturing my Davey again? You'll upset him.

[*Her hair is dyed blonde; she is trying to look ten years younger, and uses cosmetics profusely.*]

SAM: Bessie, please believe me; I tell you I'm very ill, please believe me.

BESSIE: If you say so who am I to argue. You were very ill last year and the year before that and the year before that; it's funny but every time it becomes July, you become ill as regular as clockwork. Just when everyone starts to think about holidays, he gets ill. What's the matter? Why don't you say that you don't want to take me to the seaside? And if you're so ill why won't you let me call for a doctor?

SAM: Oh, leave me alone, what do you care? You'll be able to play on your little spirit board and talk to me next week.

BESSIE: Look, Sammy, please be a good boy; it's so hot and I'm expecting Mr and Mrs Stone to tea.

SAM: How is the new Jewish Spiritualist Synagogue doing? Are you playing to full houses? Who ever heard of it? Yiddisher Spiritualism! Is there anyone there? Is it you up there Moisher: send me down a dozen pairs of nylons and five pounds of smoked salmon; I should like to see you all tapping the table for a change, instead of each other.

BESSIE: You disgust me, you old fool; and if you're going to die, please do it before tea-time because I've got a sponge-cake in the oven. [*She exits into the house.*]

　　[HAVA *comes forward.*]

SAM [*does not see her*]: Eh? Sammy? So this is what you made of your life; well, maybe it's just as well; think how difficult it would be to part for ever if you loved each other.

HAVA: Don't worry, Mr Levy, try and go to sleep.

SAM: Who's that? [*He sits up.*] Oh, it's you, Hava. Looking for your Dad?

HAVA: No, I just looked in. Miriam wasn't in.

SAM: Oh, God, life was a mistake; it shouldn't have been given to us, we didn't deserve it. The cockroaches deserve life more than human beings.

HAVA: Don't you love each other any more?

SAM: No, no more.

HAVA: Did you ever love each other?

SAM: Yes; I tell you this as a warning. I was on a steamer going to Southend for the day; she was sitting on the top deck in a white calico dress and her lovely black eyes smiled down at me, oh, so expressive. Two years later we got married, and moved to this house and after Davey was born we went shopping and bought twin beds. What went wrong? I shall never know! There is too much in life, too much to learn, not enough time. Too many problems to be solved. It's too late, now.

[DAVID *comes back into the garden; his mood has changed.*]

HAVA: Look, there's David.

[DAVID *ignores her completely as if she doesn't exist.* SAM *continues talking.*]

SAM: I used to think that the top of my head would blow off trying to answer these questions; then one day I thought that I'd grow a new head where these problems would seem like simple sums, nice pieces of cake that you could digest and get rid of easily. Hello, Davey, you met Hava, didn't you?

DAVID: I'm sorry, Dad, but a person can't help being himself. Oh? Yes, I've seen her around. [*He ignores her.*]

SAM: Hava, come here, you've met my boy, Davey, haven't you?

HAVA: Well, we never quite –

[HAVA *offers* DAVID *her hand and he shakes it limply and then continues ignoring her. She just does not exist in* DAVID'S *eyes.*

SAM *pulls David close and ruffles his hair.* HAVA *walks around the garden sometimes looking at them and sometimes looking at and sniffing the flowers.*]

Don't mind me.

SAM: We shouldn't argue, you and I. I've always loved you. You were all I really ever lived for; part of that lovely dream that slipped through my fingers. I'm sure you'll find yourself, one day, and when you do remember me and all the others who never got anywhere.

[DAVID *is sad.*]

Come on, Davey, pull yourself together; liven up, sing. Say all those crazy things I used to chastise you for saying. Spout all the things you read from books and heard from your strange friends. I want to change everything. I want something new to happen. I want to lose all sense of order, so that I'll be prepared for my new existence if there is one! Everyone where I'm going may be like you; I want my son to vouch for me in the unaccustomed darkness. Come on, Davey, 'Hurrah, hurrah'; come on, darling, spout poetry, sing, shout, come on, Davey. [*He claps his hands and so does* HAVA. SAM *has got out of bed again.*]

DAVID [*shouting*]: Listen, everyone; listen, folks. This is David Levy speaking, your master of ceremonies, your own prince of song, a prisoner of seasons, a disciple of dust. I fell out of the sky and a name fell upon me, and I was called Levy and now for a time I answer to that. My old man is going to die and so are we all before your very eyes.

HAVA: Come on, Davey, sing. I like hearing your voice.

SAM: Come on, Davey, sing.

DAVID: No! Not now. I want to speak. Tonight, friends, I'm going to launch my father into space.

SAM: Halleluia, I'm a bum; halleluia, bum again; halleluia, give us a handout to revive us again.

[*There is a general commotion in the neighbourhood; irate voices are heard and the* CHILDREN *have come on the stage and are standing around happy and delighted.*]

DAVID: This is David Levy speaking to you; I'm consigning my father to you, oh mighty dead, he is a king if ever there was one, first because he is my father, and then he is king of the herrings; to you, oh mighty dead, to you, all you billions and billions of dead who have passed this way over the earth, since it shot off from the sun, accept my father, a humble novice in this game of chance, in this maze of existence, look after him for my sake.

[MR SEGAL *enters.*]

SEGAL: What on earth are you doing? Sam, get back into bed at once, do you want to catch your death of cold?

HAVA: Daddy, please; don't interfere.

SAM: I'll die from what I choose. I'll die from playing blind man's buff if I feel like it; it's a free country; come on, kiddies, come and play with me.

SEGAL [to HAVA]: You shouldn't have let him, anyway what are you doing now? [He sees DAVID.] Don't you get mixed up with him, that's all I ask. Haven't I been a good father? Don't the things that I tell you count?

HAVA: Oh, Daddy, shut up, shush . . .

[The CHILDREN are reluctantly approaching SAM, who is beckoning them.]

SAM: Go on, sing and dance, show me how to do it.

[The CHILDREN join hands nervously.]

What games shall we play? What songs do you know?

[The CHILDREN move around in a circle.]

CHILDREN: There were three crows sat on a stone.
    Fal, la, la, la, lal, de.
    Two flew away and then there was one.
    Fal, la, la, la, lal, de.
    The other crow finding himself alone,
    Fal, la, la, la, lal, de.
    He flew away and then there was none,
    Fal, la, la, la, lal, de.

[They continue dancing around like this and SAM and HAVA join in with them. They become quieter and dance on like this whilst DAVID looks at them and sings simultaneously.]

DAVID: Sky, sky, the children cry,
    Where do we go to when we die?
    What are we doing in this dream?
    Sky, sky, the children scream,
    Sky, sky, the children scream,
    Life is nothing but a dream,

A game of dancing in a ring,
Sky, sky, the children sing.
Sky, sky, the children sing,
Who'll be beggar? Who'll be king?
Let's dance for joy, let's sing and leap,
And comfort everyone who weeps.
Sky, sky, the children weep,
Why are we falling fast asleep?
We'll play this game until we die.
Sky, sky, the children cry.

CHILDREN: He flew away and then there was none;
            Fal, la, la, la, lal, de.

[*The* CHILDREN *clap and* SAM *is encouraging them.* SEGAL *is still trying to get him back into bed, without success.*]

HAVA [*to* DAVID]: That was very nice, you can really sing.

DAVID: Who are you? Oh, yes! Thanks. [*He smiles and moves away, disinterested, before she can reply.*]

HAVA: My – I'm – Hava . . . You've got a lovely – voi . . . Oh, dear, what a life!

SAM: Come on, now, ring-a-ring-a-roses. [*He and* DAVID *now form a circle with the* CHILDREN.]

[HAVA *stands sadly near her father, watching.*]

Ring-a-ring-a-roses, a pocket full of posies,
Usher, usher, we . . . all fall . . . DOWN.

[*They all fall on the grass, and* DAVID *and the* CHILDREN *manage to get up, but* SAM *can't manage it.*]

DAVID: Come on, Dad, come back to bed.

[SAM *pushes him away with a silent gesture of his hands, crawls over to a rose-bush. He plucks enough and then he staggers to his feet; he stoops and gives a flower to each child, one to* DAVID, *which he puts into his lapel, and one to* HAVA.]

SAM: Go on now, kiddies, hide-and-seek, now we are playing hide-and-seek; run away and hide; run away, quickly get away, hide-and-seek. [*He is shouting at them and the* CHILDREN *quickly run from the garden.*]

[DAVID *and* HAVA *help* SAM *back into the bed.* SAM *settles back and is calm again.*]

Now, seriously, let's face facts, what's going to happen to you, Davey?

SEGAL: What do you mean? God forbid if anything happens to you, he'll take over the stall; he's bound to.

DAVID: Here we go again. Oh well, I know – I've had it – I'm caught – What do you want of me? Bang go my dreams, my lovely dreams, my prospects.

SEGAL: Now he's beginning to see sense. By the way, Davey, have you met my daughter . . .?

DAVID: Yes. We met.

SAM: Mr Segal, would you mind not interfering in my business; you've done so long enough.

[SEGAL *is offended and sits back and reads a newspaper, and through the next scene he is very interested, though every time* DAVID *or* SAM *looks his way he quickly reverts to the paper.*]

HAVA: Well, I'll go and see if Miriam is home yet. Good-bye, Mr Levy. Good-bye, Davey. Don't worry, everything will be all right.

SAM: Good-bye, darling . . . What a lovely g . . .

DAVID: Oh? Oh, good-bye . . . I'm sure it will.

[HAVA *kisses her father on the cheek and goes sadly off.*]

SAM: You are covered, Davey boy, I hope you realize that; I've got a special endowment for you. When I die you will get two hundred pounds. Well? You don't seem very eager, don't you want the money?

DAVID: I don't want that sort of money. Anyway, what can you do with two hundred pounds?

SAM: You can build up the business into a really posh layout; or you can take a world trip before you begin.

DAVID: Don't make me laugh, a world trip? You're living in the past. All I could do is buy a motor-scooter or eight new suits.

[*The stage is slowly getting darker, slightly.*]

Look, Dad, no one thinks for one moment that you're going to die. Nobody takes you seriously; everybody believes that you'll outlive the lot of us.

SAM: Believe it or not, I want to tell you something and I want you to make me one promise. Listen, Davey; today boys and girls go out with each other, they press against each other in doorways, under the moon, they experience a thrill and they call it love. They get married on the strength of this feeling and they still call it love. All right for a time, this new experience waking up in the morning and finding a warm, naked girl beside you in bed; but all the time the gilt is wearing off the gingerbread; soon the only time they meet is in bed and they meet there less and less. About this time the child usually comes and the woman has something to keep her occupied and the man drinks and returns to his dreams. It is too late. Time passes; they decide to make the most of a bad job. Don't settle for second best like your mother and I did. Marry a girl who shares your interests, so that when the love of passion cools down, the love of admiration and real friendship flares up and compensates; and then you have deep ties that can never be broken, not by anything. Do you understand what I mean?

DAVID: Of course.

SAM: Then promise me you'll try your best.

DAVID: Oh, Dad, why do you think . . .? Oh, never mind – I'll try.

SAM: Will you stay here when I'm dead?

DAVID: I don't know – I suppose so.

SAM: Good boy, but are you sure? I mean, be careful of your mother – She'll kill you with her love for you.

DAVID: Make up your mind – now I decide to stay you start getting cold feet.

SAM: I've got more than cold feet – I've got the screaming willies and the heeby-jeebies multiplied together. There's a great wail leaving my soul as if my body was the great wailing wall.

[*Enter* BESSIE *with* MR *and* MRS STONE.]

MR STONE: How are you, Sam?

SAM: Not so bad. How are you?

MR STONE: Mustn't grumble.

SAM: Why not? [*There is a shaking of hands all round and the guests sit down.*] How are you, Mrs Stone?

MRS STONE: All right, thank you. How are you, Bessie?

BESSIE: Don't ask me; what with one thing and another, I don't know if I'm coming or going. [*She exits into the house.* MRS STONE *nods continuously like a Chinese mandarin.*]

MRS STONE: Well, Sam, how are you feeling? Bessie tells me you have a chill.

SAM: The chill is gone, thank God; I'm going to follow it.

MRS STONE: Good, good. How are you, David? Working?

DAVID: I'm fine. I've got a job circumsizing yiddisher mice.

MRS STONE: Sounds an interesting job.

MR STONE: He's having you on.

[BESSIE *returns with a tray of tea-things.*]

BESSIE: Take no notice of him, Mrs Stone – what a life I have with that boy, no tongue can tell; there's no house like this, not another house in the world like this; all we do is argue. Oh – come on, let's all have a nice cup of tea. [*They are all seated around the small garden table that has a striped coloured umbrella above it. They sip tea and talk.*]

MR STONE: What do you think of the political situation, Sam?

SAM: What about it? [*He shrugs.*]

MRS STONE: How's Lottie, Mrs Levy?

BESSIE: She's very well, when I heard last; she's living in Leeds – of course you know. He's a school teacher up there; so I mustn't grumble. He looks after her even if he isn't a yiddisher feller. Beautiful weather we are having. How's business, Mr Stone?

MR STONE: Mustn't grumble.

SAM: Why not?

MR STONE: The taxi game never changes; too many new boys taking it up; they all think it a cushy life; they'll learn soon enough. I also stand down the Lane on Sundays now and again. I'm what you might call a purveyor of bad taste; anything that I can get my hands on I sell; you know, those horrible plaster dogs and boys eating cherries, balloons, little men running up sticks, nonsense. Give the British public something to waste money on and they cry for the opportunity. Alabaster saints and plaster ducks, oh, horrible. Mustn't grumble. Did you hear that fight the other night, Sam? Gerry Freed, the yiddisher boy from Brooklyn, got knocked out in the first round by the coloured boy. I told you so.

SAM: I don't listen to boxing any more.

SEGAL: He reads the Bible instead. Nearly all day, nearly all night.

MR STONE: And how are you, Mr Segal?

SEGAL: Why should I complain? I've got such good children: my son sends me fifty dollars a month from the States and my girl looks after me like a little mother. Have a cigar? [*He hands one to* MR STONE *and one to* SAM.] He sends these to me from America; I feel like a millionaire; still, why not? Didn't I slave long enough for them?

MRS STONE: I wish I had some children to appreciate me. I would appreciate that.

[*She looks at* MR STONE *and he pinches her cheek.*]

MR STONE [*sings*]: When your hair has turned to silver
I will love you just the same;
I will always call you sweetheart,
It will always be your name . . .

DAVID: Oh, Christ!

MR STONE: What's the matter, David? Don't you like my voice? I had a good voice when I was younger; I once won an amateur competition at the Troxy. Anyway, Sam, what's all this about you reading the Bible in your old age?

SAM: There are a couple of reasons why I started to re-read the Bible; first, I wanted to get what you may call a little spiritual comfort; I wanted to understand life a bit more.

MRS STONE: Anyway, Alf [*to her husband*], what's wrong with the Bible? Intelligent men read it, educated men, I can tell you that;

more people should read it; there wouldn't be so many black-
guards about.

DAVID: I am a blackguard and I read the Bible.

SEGAL: What's this? What's this? Sam, do you hear that? Your own
son said he was a blackshirt. You should be ashamed of yourself.

[BESSIE *hands him some cake.*]

SAM: Shut up, Davey, take no notice of him everyone, he's trying to
assert himself. Well, where was I? Oh, yes, I wanted to clear up a
few points that worried me since I was a child. Now, Adam and
Eve had only two sons: Cain and Abel; as you know Cain killed
Abel. Well, how did future generations come about? Who did
Cain sleep with, I ask you. Incest, you might think. I looked it up
yesterday and found that Cain went out into the land of Nod, and
knew his wife.

ALL: Land of Nod?

SAM: Yes, the land of Nod.

[*They all look at* MRS STONE *who has been nodding all the time.*]

MRS STONE: Why are you looking at me? What have I got to do
with it?

SAM: You see, it's allegorical.

MR STONE: Sounds like a sweet.

SAM: That's paragorical. Listen, don't interrupt; well, who was this
wife that he suddenly started to know, who wasn't even created?
Where did she come from? Was she a monkey? So what can you
believe? Then there's the Talmud, the Apocrypha, the story of
Lilith, Susanna, and the Elders; you see, none of you have heard of
these things. This is the age of the specialist; you've got to specialize,
otherwise where are you? Has anyone here heard of the Tarot
cards? The Kaballa?

[*They all shake their heads.*]

MRS STONE: Kaballa, Smaballa, leave us alone. What's the matter,
Bessie? Is he delirious? Bessie, I bought a lovely halibut for
tomorrow's dinner – Well, Bessie, how are you keeping?

BESSIE: I've got a bit of fibrositis as usual, the same as yesterday.

MR STONE: Yes, Sam, the world's in a terrible state.

DAVID: Well – Halibuts are in a terrible state – and the world's suffering from fibrositis – my old man's dying to die – my mother's got a Kaballa in the oven – all right with the world – please nod by you – The world's turning and I'm yearning to sing through the streets about my sadness and joy – Good-bye – so nice to have met you – don't call again. Charming nice son you have – tata – What a world! – What a crazy, beautiful world!

[*He goes off humming and* BESSIE *chases off after him.*]

BESSIE [*off*]: Davey – wrap up warm – it's getting chilly.

[MR *and* MRS STONE *get up and make ready to go.* BESSIE *comes on again.*]

MR STONE: Well, Sam, take it easy; I wish you better.

MRS STONE: So long, Sammy, see you some more. Good-bye, Mr Segal, take care of yourself.

BESSIE: Wheel him back into the house, Mr Segal. Don't listen to him.

[BESSIE *exits with* MR *and* MRS STONE.]

SAM: Good-bye – good-bye. Thank God for that.

[*It is getting very dark now.*]

SEGAL: Shall I wheel it in now; you heard what she said?

SAM: Segal, never be intimidated by a woman; leave me here for another half an hour. I want to see the first star in the sky. Thank you, go on now, go inside, leave me alone; we'll play cards later.

SEGAL: You know what I miss? A good game of chess; there are no chess players left in the East End. Mr Solomans and me were the champion players; I haven't played since he died last year. Where has Bessie gone?

SAM: To the spiritualist meeting with the others; they want to talk to the dead; they are fed up with the living.

SEGAL [*puffing on his cigar*]: Madame Blavatsky was an intelligent woman; I saw her once.

SAM: So was Ouspensky.

SEGAL: Rasputin was a terrible man; evil and hypnotic.

SAM: So was Ivan.

SEGAL: So was Stalin.

SAM: So they say.

SEGAL: So was Bakunin.

SAM: So was Trotsky.

SEGAL: Oh, no, Trotsky was a wonderful man.

SAM: Lenin was a wonderful man.

SEGAL: Kropotkin was a wonderful man.

SAM: My father was a wonderful man.

SEGAL: Gorki was a wonderful man, my father knew him.

SAM: Tolstoi was a wonderful man, my father never knew him. Mr Segal, do you think that there's going to be a war?

SEGAL: What do you mean? The war never finishes; the independent struggle of the individual to break his chains; the Workers themselves – and the distribution of property. In the words of our greatest comrade, 'Comrades, down with politics.'

SAM: What's the name of this greatest comrade?

SEGAL: Izzy Cohen; you know him. He's a furrier, lives in Commercial Street.

[SEGAL *exits and* HAVA *enters.*]

HAVA: Hello, Mr Levy, have you seen my father?

SAM: He's gone inside for a moment. Is it urgent?

HAVA: No. I've just come to take him home. How are you feeling?

SAM: Not too good, but I'll be better presently.

[*He seems to be in pain.*]

HAVA: You rest. It'll do you the world of good.

SAM: Do me a favour, Hava. Try to get to know my son.

HAVA: I would love to. We used to play together, but since I came back he looks right through me. I think he's a very nice boy and I wish he would speak to me; he probably thinks I'm still a child.

SAM: Maybe it's a natural reaction against women; after all, he hasn't exactly a good impression of married life. Listen. I'm going to die –

HAVA: Going to die? Please, Mr Levy, don't speak that way; you scare me. It's a lovely day, all the flowers are out –

SAM: Listen, be a good, sensible girl – I've had my time and I'm going to die – what's more natural than that? Face facts – you're a woman now.

HAVA: What will happen to David?

SAM: Try to get to know him – he's my big worry.

HAVA: If only he'd let me – I don't want to push myself – he's too busy with worrying about his voice.

SAM: But I thought you liked his voice.

HAVA: I do – I love it – but he doesn't like me. What can I do?

SAM: Take your time – there isn't a woman yet been born who let her quarry slip through her fingers – encourage him to sing if you want to – my part – but bring him down to earth – tempt him – you're just the girl he needs.

HAVA: Do you think so?

SAM: Sure – you're such a lovely girl – so attractive and good-natured – ideals are very fine but they don't keep you warm in bed – he'll fall – be patient.

HAVA: Do you really think so? Anyway – I'm not that hard up – plenty more fish in the sea.

SAM: Yes, but not such a lovely red herring like my Davey – anyway – do your best.

HAVA: I'll try.

SAM: Promise? For my sake – his sake – your sake?

HAVA: I promise. You sleep now, Mr Levy – you'll feel much better tomorrow, you'll see. I must go now and find my daddy – Are you comfortable? Can I get you something?

SAM: No, no, no. There's a good girl – Go now – you're an angel.

HAVA: Are you sure you don't need anything?

[SAM *shakes his head.* HAVA *goes off into the house.*]

SAM: Little girls are so lovely – so gentle and kind. Lots of things I need, darling, but it's too late to think about them now.

[*The* CHILDREN *start to sing again: their voices are much slower and slightly off key.*]

CHILDREN [*off*]: On the hill there stands a lady,
        Who she is I do not know.
        All she wants is gold and silver,
        All she wants is a fine young man –
  [DAVID *jumps over the garden fence and stands inconspicuously among some flowers.*]

DAVID [*sings*]: On the hill there stands a lady,
        Who she is I do not know.
        All she wants is gold and silver,
        All she wants is a fine young man.
        On the hill there stands a lady,
        Who she is I do not know,
        I have seen her often lately,
        In the sun and in the snow,
        All she wants is golden rings and silver,
        So I heard the little children sing,
        She must know that I am not a Rockefeller,
        I am skint and haven't got a thing.
        All she wants are diamonds, and all she wants are sables,
        All she wants are all the things that I could never
        Hope to give her –
        When I stretch my hands to reach her,
        Stretch my longing hands to reach her,
        The city throws its lonely streets at me.

SAM: It got dark suddenly, as if the sun fell like a stone; I thought I heard someone singing. The world would be very dark if there wasn't any light; that goes without saying. Ah, there it is, the evening star. Starlight. Starbright, first star I've seen tonight, wish I may, wish I might, grant this wish. [*He closes his eyes and makes a wish and then he opens them again and fumbles in the bedclothes for a cigarette; he lights the cigarette, puffs at it for a few moments and then throws it away.* DAVID *picks up the cigarette and smokes it.*] A funny thing has happened to me, I know it. I've been poisoned.

DAVID: Poisoned?

SAM: My heart is jumping, all the bitterness of years I can taste in my throat. I've been poisoned by someone or something. What's the odds? By my life or my wife. But my wife was my life; so my life poisoned me, so my wife poisoned me.

DAVID: She? Poisoned him? My mother?

SAM: What do I care? I don't want to live another day; die quietly, Sam, let no shame come on the name of Levy.

DAVID: He knows all about it, but is not going to reveal the truth. I will. I will. She'll see.

SAM: Who'll miss me, anyway? Caruso is dead and Chaliapin is dead; Melba is dead; Stepney Green is dead; Whitechapel is dead. What am I waiting for? Whatever became of Whitechapel? Teeming with people, so gay, so alive . . . where are they? Where are the old men with the long white beards, where are the women selling beigels? Where are the young fellers following the young ladies along the waste? Everyone I ever loved is dead, everything that was any good is dead, has been murdered.

[DAVID *hurriedly walks across the back of the garden and goes into the house.*]

SAM: Our standards are lowering; everything is dead and being put into tins, smaller and smaller, good-bye cabbages, good-bye oranges, good-bye silver fishes; everything is in tins and compressed, frozen and chopped up. We are being dried and turned inside out and we are watching ourselves in this process on little silver screens; I may as well be dead.

[DAVID *returns to the garden and is about to go over to his father when he decides against this and takes his previous position.*]

Mumma? Yes, I can hear you. Speak louder. How are you? [*He is sitting up and staring at the air.*] I am cold. Oh, rock me, Mumma, I am tired. Oh Mumma, Mumma, hold me. Where are you? Let me see, oh there you are. Come closer, closer, stand by the candles. You haven't changed. There is a long river that flows from the Minories, under Tower Bridge; it flows into the sea, but it doesn't lose itself; it flows all over the long ocean and I am swimming so easily along it – to you. To Russia, where you are standing, smiling at me; oh, Mumma, how lovely you look!

[*He climbs out of bed.*]

What's up with you, Sam? Your mind's wandering. You should be ashamed of yourself, calling for your mother.

[*He walks about the stage deliriously and by the time the next speech ends he is slumped across the bed.*]

Oy, Mumma, I remember how you used to swing me, right up into the sky, and then – down to the ground . . . I remember you singing . . . [*He sings.*]

[*Note: Song will be sung in Russian or Yiddish.*]

[*singing*]: Go to sleep, mine baby, go to sleep.

Whilst the stars above begin to peep,

Through the window of heaven, angels watch over you.

Roshenkers mit munderlun, sluft mein kinderla, sluft . . .

Oh, Mumma, look. I am crying on your apron. Let me sleep against you. I love the smell of your clothing. Oy, what can you do when you die alone?

[*He is lying spreadeagled across the bed looking upwards.* DAVID *rushes to him.*]

DAVID: Dad, listen to me; you are not alone.

SAM: If you die alone, wherever you are, what can you do?

DAVID [*shakes him*]: I tell you, Dad, you are not alone. Oh, can't you hear me?

SAM: Even if fifty people surround your bed, you die alone.

DAVID: Dad, Dad, you are not alone. This is David. I'm with you.

SAM: For when the eyes close – no one can go into that total darkness with you.

DAVID: I'm with you. Listen, Dad, I love you.

SAM: So here – goes – Sam – Lev-y poisoned by his wife or his life; a smaltz herring dealer of Wentworth Street – mourned by his d-ial-ect-ical daughter and by his crazy crooning son. Oy, oy, Shema Yisroel – Dead Mother keep me warm.

[*He dies.*]

ACT ONE

DAVID [*rushing around the stage*]: Hi, there, everyone; come out, come out, my father is dead; he is dead; he's been poisoned; for God's sake let's have some light, lights – lights . . .

[*All the lights go full on.* SEGAL *and* HAVA *rush on to the stage.* DAVID *weeps into his father's body.* SEGAL *rushes to* DAVID *and pulls him away.* HAVA *clutches at David's sleeve.*]

DAVID: Who are you? What do you want?

[HAVA *runs off the stage crying.* SEGAL *and* DAVID *stand together looking at Sam's body, unable to move. The* CHILDREN *are heard singing quietly.*]

CHILDREN: Sky, sky the children cry,
　　　　　Where do we go to when we die?
　　　　　What are we doing in this dream?
　　　　　Sky, sky, the children scream.
　　　　　SKY: SKY: SKY: SKY: SKY: SKY: SKY: SKY.
[*The word becomes louder and louder until it becomes metallic and unbearable.*]

SLOW CURTAIN

ACT TWO

SCENE 1

It is a few days later.
Late evening and the stage is almost in darkness. Only a little of the garden is seen now. Action mainly takes place in the living-room.

[*When the curtain rises a figure is seen walking slowly into the house from the garden. It walks slowly around the room, looking at things, but is not discernible; the figure then sighs audibly and slumps into an armchair.* DAVID *enters. He is dressed in a casual dark grey suit. He puts on the light and sings. The figure (*SAM*) joins in the chorus but* DAVID *at first does not notice anything.*]

DAVID: Quiet and still was the garden of Eden,
　　　Oh woe – woe is me –

TOGETHER: Oh woe – woe is me –

DAVID: God said I'll start humanity breathing,
　　　wake my baby son Adam,
　　　under the tree the serpent lay scheming,
　　　Oh – woe is me.
　　　Eve gave Adam the apple of bitterness,
　　　Oh woe – woe is me –

TOGETHER: Oh woe – woe is me –

DAVID: Guilty and sad they covered their nakedness,
　　　out of Eden they ran,
　　　far from that place they fled into nothingness,
　　　Oh woe – is me.

　　　Quiet and still is the garden of Eden,
　　　Oh woe – woe is me –

TOGETHER: Oh woe – woe is me –

DAVID: There sits the Lord alone and grieving,
        weeping over his son –
        Under the tree the serpent lies sleeping –
    [DAVID *is choked and stops singing;* SAM *continues.*]

SAM: Oh – woe is me.
    [DAVID *turns around and gasps; rushes quickly to the door and switches the light off.*]

SAM: Come on, Davey boy, don't be scared of your own father.

DAVID: I must be going out of my mind. I don't believe it. [*He switches on the light.*] But – b-b-b-but – you're dead . . .

SAM [*looking slightly better in health than he did in the previous Act and still in pyjamas*]: Believe me, I should be as scared as you, after all, it's my funeral you've just come from.

DAVID [*approaches* SAM *slowly and cautiously*]: I must be dreaming all this. That's right, I'm dreaming. I'm dreaming I'm awake. I'm dreaming that we buried you. [*He touches Sam's face, then shakes his head several times.*] No! I'm not dreaming.

SAM: Who knows who's dreaming?

DAVID: Are you – a ghost?

SAM: What's in a name?

DAVID: But you are dead.

SAM: Yes, I'm dead. It's as if I just walked in from that garden because I was cold; came in to sit down and think.

DAVID: I must be going crazy, of course he's dead. I've just come from the grounds. I threw earth on his coffin. Oh, that terrible sound of earth falling on wood.

SAM: Don't be morbid. Where are the others?

DAVID: They'll be here soon. We washed our hands and strangers filled up the hole. Daimlers brought us back. Those same cars will be fluttering with white ribbons on Sunday, carrying brides instead of corpses.

SAM: Shut up, you give me the willies.

DAVID: The shiva is starting soon. Oh, those seven days of mourn-ing. The weeping and wailing.

SAM: Arh! Weeping will do them good – let them get it all out of their systems. When I came in just now I went to look at myself, and when I saw the mirror was covered I knew definitely that I was dead.

DAVID: Why do we cover mirrors?

SAM: So that we shouldn't see our own grief.

DAVID: Why shouldn't we see our own grief?

SAM: How should I know?

[Pause.]

DAVID: Why did you come back?

SAM: To help you.

DAVID [annoyed and surprised]: What do you mean?

SAM: I only mean and know one thing: you need me.

DAVID: Don't make me laugh. [He laughs.]

SAM: You're unhappy – that's why I came; you're holding on to me.

DAVID: I'm not doing anything of the kind. Don't give me that – there's another reason – a deeper reason – you're fooling yourself.

SAM: Davey – you're all mixed up – I've come to help you settle down – I'm at your disposal.

DAVID: Help me? How can you? Besides, you can't even help yourself. Everyone knows that ghosts are displaced persons. You made a mess of your life and now you're making a mess of your death – if you want to hang around the house don't use me as an excuse. You came back because you were killed and not because I'm unhappy.

SAM: So – you admit you're unhappy – why?

DAVID: Oh! Well, because – you died too soon.

SAM: But I kept warning you.

DAVID: Yes, but I never listened and I argued with you and never amounted to anything – oh, go away.

SAM: You called me, so I'm here – everything's turning out fine.

DAVID: No, it's not. You died in very strange circumstances.

SAM: Stop depressing me. Listen, Davey – life is a very strange

circumstance; for years I told you I was going to die. Well, here I
am, or rather, here I am not.

DAVID: You're hedging – poor ghost.

SAM: 'Ere, cut that out. Don't you poor ghost me. And don't sulk.
Incidentally you've got a lovely voice.

DAVID: But only the other day you were saying exactly the opposite.

SAM: Only the other day I was exactly the opposite.

DAVID: What's it like being dead?

SAM: I can't answer that question. It's without meaning. You may
as well ask a blind man to describe the colour green.

DAVID: It's going to be just fine, I know – apart from all my other
worries, I now have a ghost on my hands – another father would
have the decency to die and to stay dead – trust you.

SAM: Davey, don't you see – I live only in your mind and heart. No
one else will see me; nobody else will want to.

DAVID: Tell me, Dad – do you believe in God?

SAM: Do I believe in God? Davey, do I believe in ghosts? Well, not
really, yet I am a ghost. Only certain people see ghosts, only certain
people want to see ghosts. You don't look into the gutter for flying
birds. Only certain people see God, only certain people want to see
Him. I want to find God and I'm still looking for Him, that's why
I believe in Him.

DAVID [recites]: I fled Him down the years and down the days –
I fled Him down the arches of the years –

SAM: Come on, Davey – don't mope – you're only young once –
let's be gay.

DAVID: Look – how can I? Especially now – don't you see you were
killed – we've got to avenge your murder.

[DAVID wanders around the room wrapped in thought.]

SAM: Murder? Oh, what's he on about now? Oh, well – listen – even
if I was killed, I don't want revenge for that, whether I was
poisoned, gassed, burned, or struck by lightning, I want revenge
for the way I lived – for the self-deception, the petty lies and silly
quarrels. Anyway, what do you mean murdered?

DAVID: Come off it – you know perfectly well that you were poisoned.

SAM: Oh, Davey – you've got it all –

DAVID: I heard you on your death-bed.

SAM: Oh – listen – I meant –

[*There is a ring on the bell.* SAM *is about to go quickly to the door when he realizes his ghostly position. He beckons* DAVID *to go.* DAVID *returns with a well-dressed young man; dressed in the manner of a City gentleman. He is wearing a bowler hat.*]

MAN: So terribly sorry to disturb you, especially at a time like this. Could I speak with Mrs Levy, please?

DAVID: My mother hasn't come back yet. Can I help you?

MAN: I'm Mr Green of the Jewish Memorial Company. I would like to wish you a long life.

[*They shake hands and* DAVID *finds in his hand a visiting-card.*]

GREEN: Excuse the slight indiscretion of coming so soon, but facts have to be faced. Your poor father will be needing a stone. We have the finest stones in the country.

SAM: He sounds like a kidney doctor.

[GREEN *takes out a book of photos and shows them to* DAVID.]

GREEN: Italian marble. Lovely green with black streaks; hard as iron. Same as Lyons Corner House.

DAVID: Look, just leave me alone. I don't think we want any today.

SAM: Oh, cheer up, Davey, you're a long time dead.

GREEN: Well, I'll just wait for your mother – she'll be more practical, more down to earth, about your poor father. [*Muses through his catalogue.*] Yes, we've got the lot – here's a nice inexpensive job – contemporary design, you know, all the rage. I've ordered one for my own mother.

SAM [*looking at the catalogue*]: Arh, it's flashy.

DAVID: Did you meet anybody on the other side?

[GREEN *looks at him strangely.*]

SAM: Not a soul – it was even somehow lonelier than my life.

DAVID: How long do you think you're going to stay?

GREEN: Until she comes.

SAM: Until you become a happy boy.

DAVID: Looks as if we're going to have you around until I'm dead also.

[*There is another ring at the door.* DAVID *shrugs and goes and returns with another man. He is wearing glasses and dressed similarly to the first man. The new man remembers that he is wearing a carnation in his buttonhole. He discards this promptly and* SAM *picks it up, smells it, and puts it into a small jug on the mantelpiece. The new man and* GREEN *frown at each other.*]

MAN: May I have a word with Mrs Levy?

DAVID: Are you a door-to-door salesman?

MAN: Indeed not.

SAM: He is, in a way.

DAVID: She's not home just yet. I'm her son.

MAN [*shakes* DAVID'S *hand violently and leaves within it a visiting-card*]: I wish you long life. I'm Mr Black of the Hebrew Remembrance Company. I want to sell your mother a beautiful memorial stone; one that would be worthy of your dear dead father. Such a fine, kind man, wouldn't harm a fly. I knew him well.

SAM: A feller of infinite jest. Never saw him before in my life, and I used to swat flies all day.

BLACK: Forgive me for coming so soon, but in the words of our motto: GET THE STONE SETTLED AND LEARN TO SMILE AGAIN.

[*He sits down near* GREEN. *They ignore each other.*]

DAVID: Look at them, how similar they are.

SAM: And look how much they hate each other.

DAVID: And you wanted me to become something like this. A nice respectable job with prospects.

SAM: God forbid. I must have been mad.

DAVID: That's what you accused me of being.

SAM: All right – don't go on, and stop arguing. That's what I seemed to do all my life. That's how I wasted it away.

DAVID: You admit, then, that I'm on the right track?

SAM: The trouble is you're not on any track – running wildly nowhere.

DAVID: What do I do? What can I do?

[GREEN *nods to* BLACK: *points a finger to his temple, suggesting that David is mad.*]

BLACK: Don't upset yourself, have a rest. You've gone through a hard time.

DAVID: Please don't tell me that everyone lives for ever.

GREEN: All right, we won't tell you that.

SAM: I should say that it's extremely unlikely. How many people would want to live for ever? Some want only to die. These two, for instance. How tired of life they must be! Already they are connected with the paraphernalia of death. They even smell of death.

[SAM *sniffs at them and* DAVID *follows suit.*]

DAVID: Yes, you're right, they do.

[*The men feel most uncomfortable.*]

SAM: When these two die, they'll swallow their own kishkers and will be dead for ever.

DAVID: Thank God for that.

GREEN: Thank God for everything. Look, son, what's your name?

DAVID: David. Why?

GREEN: Davey, listen, I'm your age, by my life. Here's my birth certificate to prove it. [*He shows* DAVID *the certificate.*] Please, you can help me; I'm not really a tombstone salesman. God forbid. I'm a feller like yourself really.

[SAM *is blowing on* BLACK'S *neck, who moves to the back of the stage and has a quiet smoke.*]

DAVID: How did you find out so soon that there'd been a death in the family?

GREEN: You're a bright boy. That's a very interesting question and I'm glad that you asked me. [*He puts his arm around* DAVID'S *shoulder.*] This is where the job is really interesting. We follow Coroners' reports, tip the porters at hospitals, make friends with mortuary keepers; check casualty lists for yiddisher names, scan obituary columns. Oh, it's a very subtle and interesting profession. Ever thought of trying it? There's a good living to be made if you're bright.

SAM: How sordid!

DAVID: I find all this very distasteful – excuse me, you see I'm not really myself. [*Turns to Sam.*] Well, what are we going to do?

GREEN [*whispers to* BLACK]: He's mad, you know – stone bonkers. I've often seen him around the streets talking to himself, everyone knows him. You may as well leave – it's a waste of time.

BLACK [*now approaches* DAVID *and takes him to one side*]: Dave, listen boy, I want to speak to you openly. Now, I don't know what that other geezer told you, but I can guess. He said his prices were more reasonable – well – it's a lie. My stone is the cheapest.

SAM: It's becoming like Hatton Garden. I should have been cremated.

BLACK [*his voice has disintegrated into Cockney*]: Look, give us a break with our unbreakable stone. Do me a favour, by my life – I should drop dead on this spot if our stone ain't the best. By my mother's life, by my father's life, by my life – I need the order – put in a good word with your mother. Look, Dave – [*He takes a photo out of his pocket and kisses it.*] Here's my wife and my baby daughter – her name's Angela – a real angel – help me earn an honest coin – I'm not really a traveller in tombstones – I'm just a yiddisher boy, like yourself, forced by circumstances to take up this vocation.

[*There is another ring at the door and* DAVID *goes. He returns, followed by a third man.*]

DAVID: I know, don't tell me – you're not really selling tombstones.

MAN: That's right – how did you guess? I'm not selling anything; as a matter of fact, I've come to give you something. Two hundred pounds for you and two hundred and fifty pounds for your mother.

DAVID: Well – please sit down.

[SAM *and* DAVID *bow him into a chair near to the other two.*]

DAVID: Well – isn't this marvellous? – I'm really mixed up now.

Suddenly I've got two hundred pounds to play with. What shall I do with it?

SAM: Remember if you keep on talking to me, they'll think you're out of your mind.

DAVID: Who cares what they think?

GREEN [*to the new man, whose name is* WHITE]: Don't be afraid of him – he's quite harmless.

BLACK: Just a bit touched in the head. Nice boy; pity.

WHITE: I've been coming to the house long enough. He hasn't changed one bit. That reminds me – [*He consults a little notebook.*] In the case of insanity I don't think we are liable to pay out on an endowment, but I can't see anything here. I'll check back to the office later. Meanwhile, I'll hold on to the money.

DAVID: I'm going to do something to really make them sit up. [*He stands on a table.*] I'll recite and wake up the world.

SAM: Don't be a bloody fool; come down here. You must grow up. You must become yourself.

DAVID: I've got it! At last! There's someone I will become.

SAM: What do you mean?

DAVID [*excited*]: Everything fits together. Why didn't I think of it before? I'm the boy with a ghost of his own. Isn't that terrific? You're my own special ghost. Before, you were only my father – now! Nothing can stop us – we're going to have a marvellous time. I've got it all worked out.

SAM: Davey – Davey – calm down – take it easy. What can I do with him?

DAVID: Don't worry, Dad – I'm doing this for you. To avenge your death – your murder.

SAM: Where do you keep on getting that idea from – I wasn't –

DAVID [*very excited*]: Listen – Shush! No time for argument – you're right – I must become myself – I must become a crazy prince to the bitter end. I can hardly wait for all that murder and chaos at the end.

SAM: Davey – just explain – what you mean.

DAVID: I'll wait until I have all the evidence and I'll strike! When everyone is dead I'll live here all alone – just crooning to the cobwebs.

[DAVID *stands in characteristic 'Hamlet' pose and* SAM *nods his head.*]

SAM: Oh – I see – Oy-vay – smir – I'll have to go along with him – otherwise – Please, Davey – I must hand it to you – a wonderful scheme – but please – take your time – and let me arrange the killings – after all, they can't hang a ghost.

DAVID: Oh – all right – but I must decide – who – when and where.

SAM: Besides, if you are the prince then I am the king.

DAVID: That's right – the king of my imagination. One minute – my mind's playing tricks on me – oh – anyway, who cares? – as long as there's a way forward into tomorrow – I wish I really knew what you really wanted of me.

SAM [*shrugs*]: I wish you knew what you wanted of yourself. Anyway, your guess is as good as mine.

[*The men are still looking at* DAVID *with astonishment.*]

DAVID: All right, my poor father – my condolences, for, for some reason, you can't rest in peace.

SAM: We make a fine pair.

DAVID: What do we do first?

SAM: First we dance and sing.

[*They chant and move together to a Jewish melody. They clap hands and dance around the rather terrified salesmen.*]

SAM: } They are not really themselves,
DAVID: } Oy, yoy, yoy, yoy, yoy.
          They are doing it for their girls,
          And their little boys.
          Tombstone selling is a job,
          Like anything else to earn a bob;
          They are not selling themselves,
          Oy, yoy, yoy, yoy, yoy.

They don't know who they are,
Oy, yoy, yoy, yoy, yoy.
On this mad demented star,
Oy, yoy, yoy, yoy, yoy.
A policy will pay the rent,
Will buy the bread and his wife's scent.
They are not really bent,
Oy, yoy, yoy, yoy, yoy.

SAM: Have a good time – don't worry – well, how do you want to begin?

DAVID: I want to stay and wait for the fireworks. I want to make them and throw them. I know! I'll dress up. I'll be unique. I'll get a great mad gimmick. I'll dye my hair red or maybe light blue.

SAM: Don't be such a silly fool. That would spoil everything.

DAVID: I'll make and break the rules just as I feel like it. I'll shock them out of their lives. There'll be no more rest for anyone from now on.

[DAVID *rushes off in a maniac state and the three men continue with the card game they have been engrossed in.*]

GREEN: Stick!

BLACK: Twist . . . oh, bust!

SAM: Schmeral.

[BESSIE *comes on, dressed in black, followed by* MR *and* MRS STONE, SEGAL, *and* HAVA, *who also are dressed in mourning.*]

SAM [*goes to Hava and forgets that he is a ghost*]: Hello, sad eyes – why are you looking so sad? Oh, I forgot – is it on account of me? Don't worry, I'm all right.

HAVA: My, it's chilly in here. The nights are drawing in. Where's Davey?

SAM: Do have a word with my boy; try to help him. He needs a nice girl like you.

HAVA: Daddy, I'll be glad when we move from Stepney Green. It's only full of memories now. All my friends are gone. It's full of bomb-sites and ghosts. It was the first funeral I ever went to.

WHITE: Mrs Levy, I would like to speak with you for a moment.

[*They go to one corner of the room, where they whisper.*]

SAM [*goes to* BESSIE]: Suddenly I'm dead – and buried. Why didn't we make a go of it? Where did our love go to? Oh, I'm not blaming you – I'm only asking.

MRS STONE: Are you feeling all right, dear?

HAVA: Yes, not too bad. Wonder where Davey is? I'd like to talk to him. Maybe he'll take me for a walk and everything will be different now.

SEGAL: Don't you worry about him. You worry about your poor old father. So, here we are back at the house, everyone here except poor old Sam.

SAM: Don't be too sure.

STONE [*goes close to his wife and places his arm around her*]: It's funny how a person you know suddenly just dies – they go into a room, a hospital, and never come out. My own mother, the last time I saw her, was in a narrow bed surrounded by flowers and fast asleep. She looked just like marble. I left the ward and five minutes later she died. She went into that place and never came out again. They wheeled the body out. A shell, a husk that resembled my mother. Where did she go to?

SEGAL: Ask me.

HAVA: I'm sure Mr Levy wouldn't want us to be morbid.

SAM: Oh darling, you're so right.

STONE: Millie, be a good girl, go and make a nice cup of tea. Come on, everyone, we mustn't get the miseries. That's what shivas are for. For friends and relations to come and try to make the family forget.

BESSIE: I'll never forget him. Never. He was such a good man. I tried. Didn't I try? Ask anyone.

SEGAL: When you've finished whispering, Bessie, remember this is a house of mourning.

[HAVA *and* MRS STONE *go off to make tea, and* BESSIE *sits on a low chair.*]

SAM: What a bloody hypocrite you are, Mr Segal. You can't wait to get your hands on my Bessie.

STONE: Where's David, Bessie?

BESSIE: Yes, where is he? Where's my Daverler? Am I the only mourner?

SEGAL: Don't upset yourself. He'll be here soon. He's probably very upset.

STONE: And why didn't Lottie come?

BESSIE: Oh, why didn't she come? Am I the only mourner for my poor dear husband, God rest his soul? Lottie didn't come. Her own father and not a word.

[HAVA *and* MRS STONE *return with tea, which they pour and hand round.*]

HAVA: I wonder why she didn't come? He was such a nice, kind man.

MRS STONE: Don't cry, Bessie. Don't waste your tears. The younger generation are not worth it. I'm glad I didn't have any kids. For what? What for? Do they appreciate you?

SEGAL: I tell you my son shows respect for me; he sends me fifty dollars a month; is that bad?

BESSIE: What can you expect? Lottie's husband is a school-teacher and, apart from being Communists, I think they are also vegetarian.

STONE: That explains it; blood is thicker than water.

BESSIE: Yes, I am the only mourner. No one ever cared for my poor husband like I did.

SAM: Why didn't you show it now and again? Still, it's easy to see things when you're not mixed up in them. Don't cry, Bessie. Once I didn't know that everything was wrong, now I know but I don't know how to put things right.

HAVA [*to Bessie*]: Don't cry, because your husband is sleeping now.

SAM: Yes, but dreaming heavy – no rest for the wicked.

HAVA: He is at rest and better off than the lot of us.

SAM: No – one minute of life is better than a million years of sleep.

HAVA: You're not the only mourner – all Stepney Green misses him.

SAM: Thank you, Hava, but real grief is very personal – Stepney Green will carry on as if nothing happened. Yes, Bessie, you are the only mourner, I think. Let me see. There was brother Harry who died in Warsaw thirty-five years ago. Izzy who deserted in the Great War and was never seen again. Jack who came to England with me and died of home-sickness and Betty who went to America and died drinking highballs in a low dive. Lottie is in Leeds and Davey is upstairs. There you are – Bessie with all her faults is the only mourner.

[*The* THREE MEN *approach Bessie and surround her with photos and catalogues.*]

SAM: Like dirty postcards.

SEGAL: Have a heart, gentlemen, this is a house of mourning.

[*Chastised, the* MEN *make ready to go, but* SEGAL *stops them.*]

SEGAL: No, no – don't go. We need you here for prayers.

[SAM *stands facing the audience; the stage gets darker; all the men stand up and face the appropriate way. They know their lines perfectly and they chant in chorus. The women sway and weep softly in the background.*]

ALL MEN: We think of those dear to us . . .

       Who are no longer with us in the body . . .

[*Their voices get softer and softer, until it is just above a whisper, and they continue with the Kaddush. Meanwhile* SAM *interpolates his own chant.*]

SAM: Hear this, all you people. Listen, children of the world, both high and low, rich and poor; I shall speak the truth.

ALL: Death does not sever the bonds of devotion which unite loving hearts.

       Oh God, we ever accept your goodness and greatness.

[*They all start davening in unison until they are a swaying wave of bodies; the stage is getting darker and darker.*]

       Praise be His great name for ever and ever.

SAM: God will redeem my soul from the grasp of the grave.

ALL: Let Him be glorified and exalted –

[*All move together, softly and loudly; up and down goes the chant of voices. The women weep.*]

He will grant peace unto Israel and all mankind.

SAM: For He alone can grant peace.

May He who is the source of strength grant comfort to those in sorrow and peace to the heart of all His children.

[*DAVID enters. He is dressed in a white shirt, black tapering trousers, and a bootlace for a tie; he is now what is termed a TEDDY BOY but the similarity to Hamlet must be stressed. He jumps upon a sideboard. They all gasp and are shocked.*]

DAVID [*sings*]: Yiddisher father,
> I bet he misses Matzo Bry,
> Cheesecake and Smoked Salmon,
> I hope he finds some in the sky,
> Will you look at them here,
> As they stand and pray.
> When they're all very glad that he's out of the way.
> Oh my wonderful yiddisher father –
> Somebody will have to pay.

[*He points dramatically at his mother as* THE LIGHTS FADE.]

CURTAIN

SCENE 2

When the lights come up a week has apparently passed.

[*All the characters are placed exactly as before, except* SAM, *who is lying on the floor. The mirrors are uncovered and the three* MEN *are playing cards.*

BESSIE *and* DAVID *get up from their low chairs.* DAVID *is obviously in a very agitated state but is very excited and manic still. Everyone seems completely tired out – as if he had been driving them right out of their wits.*]

DAVID: Well – I'm glad that ritual's over – now my little drama can begin.

MRS STONE: David – do me a favour – do us all a favour – don't go on any more. I can't stand it. What's the matter? Aren't you happy? Don't you sleep well?

BESSIE: You've been driving us mad for a week; now take off those ridiculous clothes and put something decent on. What am I going to do with him?

SOLLY: What's he going to do with us?

DAVID: You'll find out. No – I'm sticking to these clothes.

BESSIE: But why?

DAVID: They make me feel good.

MRS STONE: I don't like saying this, Bessie, but your boy is meshuga. Why do you let him go on like this?

BESSIE [*sings to tune* Tum Balaloyka]:

> Listen, Davey, listen to me,
> What a bad boy you turned out to be,
> Driving me crazy, fast to my grave,
> Killing me, darling, can't you behave?
>
> Other mothers see joy from their child,
> You are thoughtless, hopeless and wild,
> Didn't I bring you into this life?
> Do me a favour – go get a wife.
>
> Oy-yoy-yoy-yoy – what have I done
> To deserve such a terrible son?
> Driving me frantic, driving me mad,
> Oh my dear Dave – you're just like your dad.

[*She slaps him lightly upon the face, and makes a gesture as if she could kill him.*]

BESSIE: Davey – you're killing me.

DAVID: Leave me alone.

BESSIE: I'll be dead and you'll be sorry.

DAVID: You talk too much.

BESSIE: You only have one mother – one mother!

DAVID: Thank God for that.

BESSIE: You'll cry – you'll see – when I'm gone – you don't know when you've got it good. Didn't I give you everything you wanted?

DAVID: You gave me everything you thought I wanted.

BESSIE: Tell me what you want now – I'll give it to you – if it's not too dear – don't you love your mother?

DAVID: What's love? How can I recognize it? I never saw any in this house.

BESSIE: There he goes again – clever dick. Didn't I give you enough food? [*She pinches his face.*] Come on, darling –

DAVID [*embarrassed*]: Oh – get away from me.

BESSIE [*she pinches him harder*]: I could kill him. [*She turns to Mrs Stone.*] What can I do with him?

MRS STONE: He'll grow out of it – anyway, who cares what he's like as long as he's a nice boy?

[DAVID *sweeps around the stage and booms out; they all look at him.*]

DAVID: To be or not to bloody well be, believe me, that is the question! Whether it is besser to ne a bisle meshuga –

WHITE: Twist.

DAVID: Or to take alms for the love of Allah. To kick the bucket or to take forty winks.

[*All look entranced at the boy.* SAM *wakes up.*]

STONE: He should have been an Hector.

BLACK: BUST!

GREEN: Pay twenty-ones – five cards and pontoons only.

WHITE: Pay me, then.

DAVID: To take forty vinks no more and by Ali Abracadabra to end the sourous and the hire purchase, please God by you.

[BESSIE *and* SEGAL *are flirting in a corner.*]

DAVID: These are the consumer goods for the frum yids. To kick the bucket, to take a nap at the race-track – ah! there's the snag, for on that slip of paper what names were written – blown away by the wind – blown away, etcetera, you should live so long.

STONE: Davey! I've got it all worked out. You team up with Prince Monologue and together you sell tips and sing your philosophy to the boys down the lane.

DAVID: Oh, pipe down! [*He turns to Segal.*] And you watch yourself.

SEGAL: What do you mean?

DAVID: If you must carry on like that with my mother – at least wait until my father is cold.

SEGAL: You must have more respect for older people.

DAVID: Respect! What a dirty word that is. Look, we haven't even taken the memorial light from the mantelpiece – when's the wedding?

SEGAL: What are you talking about? I was being sympathetic.

BESSIE: Darling! Davey! How could you? Please, shut up. Do me a favour – be a nice boy. LEAVE HOME.

DAVID: Look – you drove him to the grave and there he is!

[DAVID *points to Sam, who laughs, and all the others look incredulously on.*]

DAVID: No, I'm staying – staying here.

BESSIE: As a matter of fact, we were discussing the details of getting rid of your father's business.

DAVID: Getting rid of it? Oh no, you're not. That herring stall is the kingdom I've inherited. I am THE PRINCE OF HERRINGS. I'm starting work there next Monday. The smell of those little silver fishes will follow me wherever I go. I've seen millions of them one way and another and I'll see millions more. I've brushed those sticky scales from my suits a thousand times. I've watched you cut their heads off and gut them – I've seen you souse them and smaltz them, pickle them and grill them. I've dreamed of them – had nightmares about them. Millions and millions of herrings, all with the same face; kippers, bucklings, bristlings – all my loyal subjects.

SAM: Don't work down the market – plenty of time – don't rush into things. Get that two hundred pounds and go to auditions. I've got faith in you. But I must say herrings are delicious – try one, one day. I even used to eat them now and again. They have a very high vitamin yield.

BESSIE: And what's wrong with herrings? Everything in this house has been bought by them. This table – that pack of cards – your bed upstairs – your clothes – the holidays at Cliftonville.

HAVA: David didn't mean – you see, he's got other fish to fry.
  [MR STONE *laughs*.]

DAVID [*to Sam*]: Honestly! If you had your time over again, which way would you choose to earn a living?

STONE: Well – er – let me see.

SAM: I would probably do exactly the same. I make no excuses. A ghost can't afford to.

HAVA: I would like to have married – a great man – a great singer – like someone I know.

STONE: I would have liked to have been a lawyer.

SEGAL: I would have liked to have been the leader of the greatest political party in the world and a diamond merchant in my spare time.

MRS STONE: I would like to have been a ballet dancer.

BESSIE: I would have liked to have married a Rothschild.

WHITE: Stick. I would have liked to be Joe Lyons.

BLACK: I would have liked to have been an Epstein. Bust.

GREEN: Pay pontoons only. I would have liked to be a Rabbi; you see this is not my real work.

ALL [*except* SAM]: And you? What would you like to be?

DAVID: The same as I am. Prince of the Herrings. Prince Hamlet . . .
  [*They all laugh*.]

HAVA: I would like to go to the cinema. Coming, anyone?
  [*She quickly kisses her father and hurriedly exits*.]

SAM: Listen, Boychick. Hamlet wasn't an important man. Where would he have been if Shakespeare didn't rescue him from obscurity? Now Shakespeare was a different kettle of fish.

DAVID: You know everything! First I must sell herrings and then I mustn't sell herrings – then I had a terrible voice and now I've a lovely voice – make up your mind.

SAM: Why shouldn't I change my mind? Why should ghosts be different from people?

DAVID: Arh, you're not a very successful ghost – you don't bother anyone – except me.

SAM: I'm doing my work properly – if you've any complaints – you'd better get in touch with my union.

DAVID: It's all very well for you to be frivolous.

[*The telephone rings; several rush to lift the receiver but* BESSIE *beats all of them.*]

BESSIE: Hello! Yes! Speaking! Who's that? Lottie? Is that you, Lottie? Darling! [*She talks now to the room.*] Mrs Stone, my Lottie's on the phone – all the way from Leeds – Hello, Dolly – speak louder – [*to David now*] Davey – your sister's on the line – come and say hello.

DAVID: Oh – do me a favour.

BESSIE: He won't even say hello to his own sister – what do you think of that? The trouble I have with that boy – what's that, darling? – no, he hasn't changed –

DAVID: Stop talking about me and carry on talking about nothing –

BESSIE: He's mad – he's mad – his own sister – believe me, Lottie – you're better off in Leeds.

[DAVID *stomps off into the kitchen.*]

BESSIE: He's gone out of the room now – into the kitchen – how do I know? Well, how are you, darling? Good – you should be ashamed of yourself. What? No! Where? Yes – listen. Lottie – you should be ashamed of yourself – your own father – your own flesh and blood and you never came – after all the years he slaved for you – what? I can't hear! You want to speak to Davey? [*Shouts towards kitchen*] Davey – Lottie wants a word with you.

DAVID [*off*]: I'm busy.

BESSIE [*into phone*]: He's busy – always busy – he's driving us mad – no tongue can tell what I have to put up with – there's no other house like this house – you bad girl – Lottie – why didn't you even come to the shiva? What? Going to have another one? When? That husband of yours – oh, such bad news – it always comes together — Mazeltoff, darling – kiss the babies for me – wrap up warm – take care – there are the pips – you should be ashamed – good-bye, Dolly – teta! Take care – I'm all right – there're the pips – the pips – I'm all right – I'll survive somehow – Teta, Lottie! [*She puts the phone down.*] She's going to have another baby. Davey! You're going to be an uncle again!

DAVID [*off*]: Hurray!

MRS STONE: How many will this make?

BESSIE [*proudly*]: This will be my fifth grandchild.

MRS STONE: Hasn't she heard of them new clinics? Nobody goes in for big families any more.

BESSIE: Her husband is a Catholic.

SEGAL: Not long ago – you said he was a Communist.

BESSIE: He is a Communist and a Catholic.

MRS STONE [*sings suddenly*]: To sigh for you – to cry for you – yes – even die for you – that's what God made mothers for –

BESSIE: Believe me – you're right.

[DAVID *comes on, drinking.*]

SAM: What are you drinking?

DAVID: Chocolate.

SAM: Good – it was the magical drink of the Aztec gods – anyway, it won't do you any harm.

DAVID: No more smoozing me – something has got to happen soon – I must get revenge – they killed you and you won't directly admit it. WHY? You're getting cold feet – you can't rely on your own father – not even when he's a ghost. LOOK AT THEM! Just look at them!

BESSIE: We ruined him – he's feeling like this because he's got to face up to reality. He hasn't worked properly for years. He read too many books. We gave him everything he wanted. The boy with the ever-open hand. Money for jazz records – money for clothes – money for jam. He used to bring back stray dogs and mangy cats.

MRS STONE: Mangy cats?

BESSIE: I put up with a lot to stop him being a low-life. He even kept lizards as pets.

MRS STONE: LIZARDS! Oh, Bessie – how you must have suffered!

BESSIE: It was all Sam's fault. He was too soft with him.

SAM: Go on, blame the dead – how convenient a corpse can be! Why did I marry such a woman?

DAVID: But Dad – surely you loved her once.

SAM: Yes – once. [BESSIE *is eating and stuffing herself with chocolates.*]

DAVID [*to Bessie*]: Why didn't you love Dad? He was such a good man.

[*Bessie nearly chokes with a chocolate.*]

SAM: SHUT UP, DAVEY! I had my faults. Things happen between husband and wife that no one else can know about.

BESSIE: Listen to who's talking. The pot calls the kettle black. I'm going to tell you a few things about Sam –

SAM: Change the subject quick. Otherwise you'll end up by sympathizing with her.

DAVID: Mind your own business. You're no help to me. I want revenge and I want it NOW!

SAM: Davey – calm down.

DAVID: Calm! Calm, he says. You were murdered by some people in this room – and they're going to pay. I've got to avenge the injustice and the scandal.

SAM: Who in this room? What are you talking about?

DAVID: When you died you said she poisoned you – I heard you –

SAM: Oh, don't be so silly.

DAVID: It's no good backing out of it now – with my own ears I heard your last words.

SAM: Oh! I didn't really mean that she poisoned me – what I meant to say was that my life poisoned me and because once she was my life – well –

DAVID: You just said 'She poisoned me' and that's good enough for me. I know why she did – they planned it together – she and that little Soppy Segal [*points at the frightened Solly*].

SAM: You only heard what you wanted to. What was in your mind to pick out.

DAVID: You're a liar! You were telling the truth then, but now you're covering up for them – for some reason.

SAM: Davey – don't be dramatic – settle down like a good boy and learn from my mistakes. Listen, before I didn't know just how much of a mess I made of my life – now I know – but how can I get through to you? – please listen to me.

DAVID: There's only one thing I know or want to know – you were poisoned whether you admit it or not and my sole aim is to avenge your murder – I'm going to do this with or without your help – they've got to pay – anyway, before you promised to help me – well – you'd better make up your mind once and for all.

[*He goes into the garden.*]

SAM [*reluctantly*]: Very well – I have no choice. I'll have to play along with him.

[DAVID *sulks in the garden.*]

BESSIE: I did love Sam. Yes, I did – I know we didn't get on, but he was a good man and I'm going to miss him so much.

SAM: Poor Bessie – argument was the only way we could stay close. She wasn't a bad girl and if I wasn't a ghost I could get quite carried away and forgive her for everything. ALMOST.

[SAM *follows David into the garden; he goes through wall.* SOLLY *goes into garden.*]

CHILDREN: Silly Solly Segal, nose like an eagle,

      Eyes like two jelly-fish, teeth like a weasel.

[SEGAL *sits down near* SAM *and* DAVID. *The lights in the house go dim.*]

SAM: Davey – Please, what's the matter with you?

DAVID: To tell you the truth – I'm unhappy.

SOLLY: Oh, cheer up, my boy – growing up is hard.

SAM: Why? I know that most of the past was undesirable, but now we must look forward.

DAVID: I wanted so much to please you.

SOLLY: Well, that's very nice of you.

DAVID: It looks like we have permanent guests.

SEGAL: Yes.

DAVID: I wasn't speaking to you.

SEGAL: I wish you would sometimes. I might be able to give you some advice.

DAVID: I wanted you to be proud of me.

SAM: There's still time.

DAVID [mood changes]: Now that my dad's out of the way I suppose you'll marry my mother.

SEGAL: I'm lonely. Don't think too badly of me. You're too young to understand loneliness.

DAVID: Am I? Yes, ever since you died the house has been full of people.

SEGAL [jumps up]: Ever since I died? [Feels his face.] What do you mean?

SAM: Poor old boy. Don't be too hard on him.

DAVID: Every time you talk I get the feeling that it's myself thinking. My other self.

SEGAL: That's a good thing. I could teach you a lot. Politics and economics. Syndicalism. The theories of capital and labour . . .

DAVID: I was with you when you died.

SEGAL: When I died! Oh, you're driving me mad.

SAM: I'm happy to know I didn't die alone. Was it difficult seeing me die?

DAVID: Yes.

SEGAL: What do you mean? Yes?

SAM: Did I call for Bessie?

DAVID: No.

SEGAL: What do you mean? Yes! No!

DAVID: I told you – you said you'd been poisoned.

SEGAL: Poisoned? [*He staggers for a moment and splutters.*]

DAVID: Not you – not yet. [*To Sam*] I can't get over it: your best friend and your wife, glad to get you out of the way.

SAM: The real motives in people's minds are terrible things to discover; yours for instance. Don't look too deeply.

SEGAL: Poor Sam – what a responsibility being your father – is it worth it?

DAVID: Coming in? I'm feeling cold.

SEGAL: No – I want to think.

SAM: No – I want to stop thinking. When I'm with you I think too much.

[DAVID *goes inside house and sits alone.*]

SAM [*looks at Solly*]: Poor Solly.

SEGAL [*looks up*]: Poor Sammy.

SAM: Bloody hypocrite. Still, Solly wasn't a bad man – sometimes.

SEGAL [*a reprise of the duologue in Act I*]: Sammy was a wonderful man; I never really knew him.

SAM: The boy's restless and it's up to me. There must be a solution. Anyway, that's what I'm here for.

SEGAL: He was so kind.

SAM: I can't leave until I help him see straight.

SEGAL: Poor David. His mother will kill him, if they live alone. He needs a man – a great man – someone to look up to – what am I saying? He needs someone like me; I'll be a real father to him.

SAM: Bloody cheek. One minute. You're right. You're right! I hate to say this but you're right. That's the answer.

SEGAL: It's getting windy. Think I'll go in and maybe talk to Bessie.

[*As he moves to go in, the* CHILDREN *come and call after him again.*]

CHILDREN: Soppy Solly Seagull, nose like an eagle,

Eyes like two jelly-fish –

[*With a gesture of dismay he chases them and then goes into the house.*]

SAM: Mr Segal, I could k – iss you. [*Pause.*] All right, if you and Bessie get married, but I know what will happen: you'll discuss it for years, you'll argue – you'll say not enough time has passed since my burial – I've got to think of some way to get you married as soon as possible –

[*He goes through the wall again into the house and the lights go up.*]

DAVID [*rushing to* SAM *and pointing to* SOLLY *and* BESSIE, *who are now whispering together*]: You know, of course, what they're planning.

SAM [*joking*]: Are they planning more horrible murders?

DAVID: Not yet. Now they're planning to get married.

SAM Do you think I'm blind? This is a wonderful idea; you must encourage their romance if you want revenge.

DAVID: What do you mean?

SAM: Their marriage would prove they wanted me out of the way – it would prove your theories correct.

DAVID: Yeah! You're right. You're dead right.

SAM: You said it.

WHITE [*from card table*]: Listen, young man – I'm staying round to check your sanity – well, my report won't be very favourable. Our company need not pay your endowment if you're stone bonkers.

DAVID [*to Sam*]: You signed this policy knowing this clause?

SAM: Who reads policies when they sign them? Who has that much time to waste? Anyway, I signed when you were one year old – I didn't know you'd grow up to be a madman.

[MR STONE *suddenly stands up.*]

MR STONE: Well, isn't that a coincidence? Listen, everybody, their names are not really White, Black, and Green! This is really Mr Blackstone, this is really Mr Whitestone, and this is really Mr Greenstone, and I changed my name by deed poll from Goldstone to Stone.

DAVID: They dropped the stone and you picked it up.

[MR STONE *sits down and the three* MEN *stand up.*]

WHITE: In business it's better –

BLACK: It's brief and to the point.

GREEN: It pays to have a simple name.

[*The three* MEN *get into line and sing a smart clipped song; the tune is a variant of the post-horn gallop.*]

MEN: Mr White, Mr Black, Mr Green,
    Our tombstones are simply serene,
    Our companies never look back,
    Mr White, Mr Green, Mr Black.
    Mr Green, Mr Black, Mr White,
    Our companies soon set it right,
    And they're guaranteed not to crack,
    Mr Green, Mr White, Mr Black.
    Mr Black, Mr Green, Mr White,
    Insurance and tombstones are right;
    Buy British and always fight clean,
    Mr Black, Mr White, Mr Green.

[*They sit down again and play cards.*]

MRS STONE [*suddenly sings*]: You die if you worry, you die if you don't – so why worry at all? It's only worry that killed the cat, anybody can tell you that – That's funny – I feel like singing tonight. My mother used to sing that song, and do you know what? She died worrying just the same.

[SEGAL, MRS STONE, *and* BESSIE *are seated around the table.* DAVID *and* SAM *are talking quietly.*]

BESSIE: Shall we begin? Have you got the letters ready?

[MRS STONE *starts arranging letters around the table.* BESSIE *returns to the table with a tumbler.*]

MRS STONE: Come on, Alf, we're ready to begin.

[*She almost has to pull him away from the card game.*]

SEGAL: What's the matter? What's everyone gone quiet for?

BESSIE: Why, the seance, of course.

SEGAL: Who do you want to talk with?

BESSIE: Anyone who's interested in talking to us!

SEGAL: Sounds like a Summit Conference. I hope you don't pick up Sam on the high frequency.

SAM: Oh – he's sensitive.

SEGAL: Oy – the spirits – what they say is sacred – leave them alone.

[SEGAL *is about to place his arm around Bessie when he has a change of heart.*]

SEGAL [*looking at the ceiling*]: Sam – oy – Sam, forgive me, my thoughts are not nice – but my intentions are pure.

SAM: At last! I've got it. The answer.

DAVID: Look at that little hypocrite – I could kill him now.

SAM: Be patient and wait a little while. They'll kill each other.

DAVID: I want them to die – like you. No, not like you. Oh, I don't care how they die.

SAM: I'll help you kill them in such a way that they won't affect you any more. You'll be free and no one will charge you with anything. Just be patient. It's all clicked into place – this is how we get them married. [*He whispers to* DAVID, *who laughs.*]

DAVID: And once they're married, Bob's your uncle.

SEGAL: I'm filled with remorse. He was right – for once that mad man, my stepson-in-law, please God, was right – my thoughts are not becoming to a citizen of the world.

BESSIE: What are you muttering about, Mr Segal?

SEGAL: Bessie, how many years have you known me?

BESSIE: About thirty or forty years.

SEGAL: Isn't it time you called me Solly?

SAM: Here we go, Davey.

[BESSIE *smiles and places* SEGAL'*s finger on the tumbler, as the others have done.*]

BESSIE [*whispers*]: Solly, boy, are you comfortable?

STONE: Is there anyone there who wants to speak with anyone here?

[SAM *is laughing his head off, nods, and begins to move the tumbler to various letters. Everyone follows with great concentration the journey of the glass. The* MEN *at the table continue playing cards, totally unaware of the things going on.*]

SAM [*saying the word that he is spelling out*]: HITLER.

[*There is great confusion in the room as the women scream and rush as far from the table as possible.*]

MRS STONE: Oy, what do we do now? Send him back? Send him back, Alf.

BESSIE [*creeps back to the table*]: Let's ignore him and try to get somewhere else.

STONE: You never know what will turn up.

SEGAL: Maybe he just wants to apologize.

DAVID [*who pretends that he didn't see the message*]: What was the message?

STONE: It just said HITLER. Come on, let's try again. Maybe we didn't write the letters clearly enough or they're short-sighted over there.

[*They repeat the process, and* SAM, *who has been reading the sporting page of the newspaper, begins to move the glass again.*]

DAVID: What does it say now?

BESSIE: Hush.

MRS STONE: Shush.

SEGAL: Hush? Shush? What does that mean? It goes too fast. I can't read upside down.

[SAM *spells out the words again.*]

SAM: RED CLOUD . . . TWO-THIRTY . . . TOMORROW . . .

[*They all repeat this as they read the message.*]

SEGAL: Red cloud? Sounds like a Communist pirate.

BESSIE: Look, there it goes again. Red, cloud, tomorrow, two-thirty. It must be the spirit guide. You know what I mean? White cloud! Red cloud! They're always Red Indians.

MRS STONE: Why?

BESSIE: How should I know?

SEGAL [*sings*]: Red cloud in the sunset . . .

DAVID [*sings*]: Mushrooms on the sea . . .

STONE: One moment: did it say Red Cloud? [*He looks at the back page of the newspaper.*] Here it is: Red Cloud running in the big race, two-thirty tomorrow: 100 to 1.

[*He rushes to the phone and dials.*]

MRS STONE: Izzy Posner won't be there at this hour.

STONE: Izzy never leaves the office; that's his motto. Hello? Is that you, Izzy? This is me: Alf Stone. Five pounds each way, Red Cloud, two-thirty – never mind, do what I tell you.

[*At this moment the three* MEN *quickly leave the card game and rush for the telephone. One snatches it from Mr Stone and each in turn pulls it from the others; each retains it long enough only to speak his name.*]

MEN: MR WHITE. MR BLACK. MR GREEN. MR BLACK. MR WHITE. GREEN. WHITE. BLACK. WHITE. BLACK. GREEN.

[*The names coagulate into a jumble of sound. At the telephone the* MEN *continue at the action, only the sound has faded and they play in dumb show.* SAM *starts spelling out again and they follow the glass with rapt attention.*]

SAM [*spelling out the letters he is moving the glass to*]: This is – Sam – Levy . . . I forgive you, Mr Segal – take care of – my Bessie . . .

[*Everyone cheers.* SEGAL *is ecstatic and kisses* BESSIE, *and* DAVID *and* SAM *shake hands.* DAVID *looks at* BESSIE *and* SEGAL, *and rubs his hands.*]

CURTAIN

ACT THREE

Eight months later.

It is a fine afternoon in early spring; in the house there is a festive tone, that completely contrasts with the previous scene. There are flowers everywhere and the table is set with a large white tablecloth; there are bottles of wine and dishes of fruit everywhere.

[DAVID *is sitting on a chair in the garden, looking more like Hamlet and very morose; dressed in teddy boy's clothing;* SAM *is lying on the grass looking up at the sky.* CHILDREN *are playing nearby and are singing.*]

CHILDREN: Poor Jenny is a-weeping, a-weeping, a-weeping.
Poor Jenny is a-weeping on a bright summer's day.
Stand up, stand up, on your heels,
Choose the one you like the best, a lady or a gentleman;
Now you're married we wish you joy,
First a girl and then a boy.
Kiss her once, kiss her twice,
Kiss her three times over.

[SAM *gets up and does some gardening, digging, and the scene fades slightly. The* THREE SALESMEN *enter and immediately go to the table where they start helping themselves to sandwiches.*]

WHITE: You'll be happy to know that I sold her a stone; clinched the deal just before she got married.

BLACK: But you're an insurance man.

WHITE: I was an insurance man; I've now started my own little monumental stone company. By the way, why not work for me, the two of you?

BLACK: I'm afraid that's impossible. You see, I've been an insurance agent for several months.

GREEN: So am I. That's strange. I came here today to sell her an insurance policy for her husband.

BLACK: So did I and at the same time to try and get that son of hers to take out a life insurance.

GREEN: There seems to be a close parallel in our lives.

BLACK: There certainly does. Where were you educated?

GREEN: Jew's Free School. Where were you?

BLACK: Why, at the same school. Who was your teacher?

GREEN: Mr Rosen. Yours?

BLACK: Rosen also. What year?

GREEN: About 1940 I left.

BLACK: So did I. We must have been there at the same time.

GREEN: Do you like football?

BLACK: No. Do you like cricket?

GREEN: Yes.

BLACK: So do I. What a coincidence!

GREEN: Do you like me?

BLACK: No. Do you like me?

GREEN: No. How wonderful! [*They shake hands and are all smiles.*]

GREEN [*to White*]: Could you get your company to settle the David Levy claim? That is to say, your old company.

WHITE: I believe that they're doing it today. I sold Mrs Levy a stone on that understanding. I'll call in there and get the money for him.

BLACK: Tell me, what company do you represent?

GREEN: The Providential Life of Mile End.

BLACK [*excited and thrilled*]: How do you do? So do I. [*They shake hands excitedly.*]

WHITE: Did you say the Providential Life of Mile End?
    [*They nod.*]
Why, that's the company I used to work for; this calls for a drink. [*Opens a bottle and they all have a drink.*]

GREEN: Tell me, aren't you a little off your territory?

BLACK: I don't think so. My zone starts at Silvertown, extends all along Commercial Road, Watney Street, Hessle Street, Cable Street, Jubilee Street, Redmans Road, and all the area of Stepney Green, southern side.

GREEN: Let me see, my area begins at Bishopsgate, Houndsditch, Commercial Street, Brady Street Buildings, Old Montague Street, and Stepney Green, northern side. Bow Road right up to Stratford.

BLACK: There you are, you said northern side. Sorry old chap, this is the southern side. You're on my territory; David Levy is mine.

GREEN: I'm so terribly sorry, no hard feelings?

BLACK: Certainly not. Let's all have a drink.

- [*They all drink and then* WHITE *and* GREEN *make to exit.*]

GREEN: See you at the office one day. So long.

BLACK: Yes, rather. Who knows, we may see each other quite often. Bye-bye.

[GREEN *exits.* WHITE *is about to leave also.*]

Don't forget to bring him the money today.

WHITE: I shan't. So long, old boy. [*He exits.*]

[BLACK *walks smugly around the stage and starts drinking at the table. He sits down and drinks quite a lot.*]

SAM: Oh, I'm so tired; I feel like I could just sleep and sleep.

DAVID: Why don't you? You always said you deserved a rest – well, here it is.

SAM: I'm worried about you. It's about time you made up your mind? Are you going to look after the barrow or not?

DAVID: I've been in for about ten auditions in the past couple of months. You've got to have a gimmick or influence or both. I've borrowed almost the whole of that two hundred pounds from Mum; it's coming today, but I shan't get any of it. What is going to be the outcome of all this? I mean, what are you going to do? You can't stay here all your life.

SAM: All my life?

DAVID: I mean all your death. It's getting to the state where I'm beginning to think that I'm your father. What are you waiting for now?

SAM: There was the question of revenge and your future that brought me here. I think the two are really same problem. You must really make up your mind. Do you know that ever since I've been dead I haven't seen anyone over there.

DAVID: You know, of course, what happened today? Today is the big day. The day we've been waiting for.

SAM: I haven't been around so much recently.

DAVID: That's right. Where have you been going? A fine ghost you turned out to be. Why, I've almost got to like Segal in your absence. And when you're here you sleep all the time. Today is my day. I'm free either way. I'll kill myself along with the rest.

SAM [*who hasn't been listening*]: Oh, I've been wandering here and there. I went down the Lane to see all the boys. Solly Segal was there selling herrings at my stall. Then I took a boat trip to Putney and I went to the Tower of London. I walked through the front entrance of Buckingham Palace and strolled right through the place. I didn't see not one member of the Royal Family. I also went on a conducted tour with some wealthy Yanks. Hampton Court, Kew, Greenwich, Ken Wood. Davey, why didn't you tell me that London was so beautiful? What a wonderful history it has. It's like a wonderful woman you can live with your whole life and miss the entire point. It's not so bad being dead after all. I saw the city in the early morning, before anyone gets up to go to work. I walked along the riverside: it's very lovely with the sun rising with the mist, rising over the office blocks and the warehouses. I saw the swans wake up and preen themselves in the mud.

DAVID: You know, of course, what happened today. You're evading the issue. You don't want to leave here.

SAM: Being dead has great advantages. Why I even got the best seat in the Festival Hall for nothing, but I suppose it's no use; being dead like this is so impermanent. There's no future in it, don't you agree?

DAVID: You do know what happened today?

SAM: Yes, my Bessie got married.

DAVID: Does that let you out?

SAM: I suppose it must do. Segal is my exit visa.

DAVID: You're still going to help me play it out to the end?

SAM: If you're determined, I suppose so. How do you want them to die?

DAVID: The same way that you died. By poison.

SAM: Fine. Presently I'll give you a list of various ingredients needed. I want you to go out and buy them at the chemist and greengrocer. I want you to mix the concoction to my specification and then you administer it in your own time. Oh well, this is it. Everything is resolved today.

DAVID: What is the purpose in life? It seems senseless to me.

SAM: The purpose in life is to be aware that that question exists. What is the purpose in life? I wonder. I was borrowed from the darkness by your desire. I've been allowed to slip away for a few moments. I never had roots anywhere, Davey, and I'm still wandering. I love London so much that I hate leaving it, for ever and ever. If being a ghost means having a real pain in the heart then I am the biggest and most successful ghost that ever was. But I have the even greater desire to look for some other light; a light brighter than earth, a light I heard about in symphonies and poetry. I am dead and buried and live only in the imagination of a neurotic young man; you are fickle, you'll forget all about this, then I'll be really dead.

DAVID: Never.

SAM: Yes you will, and quite right too. I, Samuel Levy, of no fixed abode am being charged with loitering and soon I must leave London for ever.

DAVID: In spite of your words I'm happy. In a strange way you make me feel wonderful. I don't seem to want revenge so much.

SAM: Oh yes, you do. When you get revenge in this house, everything will turn out all right, just as it should be. But don't be too confident; you'll be hurt over and over again, and always about the same things.

DAVID: I feel I can face everything. As if I'd been taken by the ankles and battered against a wall; bashed to pulp and yet I can stand up and sing.

SAM: You still haven't grown out of that?

DAVID: I want to sing. I've got to. When I stop I'll lay down and die.

SAM: Where will you go when all this revenge business is settled?

DAVID: I'm not sure. It's been nice of you to help me.

SAM: I'm glad that I could help you, because now instead of only being your father, we are close friends. It's so easy to make a child and so hard to make a friend. Where will you go?

DAVID: Anywhere – everywhere! A grand tour – New York, Mexico, Peru, New Guinea, Siam, China, India. Come on, Dad, let me have that prescription.

SAM: Don't be in too much of a hurry. I haven't finished talking yet.

DAVID: What do you mean?

SAM: Some people never leave home; even when they put a thousand miles between them and the street door; when you leave, really leave.

DAVID: Don't start lecturing me again. We've been having a wonderful time. Don't start getting stuffy now.

SAM: Forgive me, but I think that my time is drawing near; I'm beginning to feel like a ghost should; restless and forgetful. I feel guilty and uncomfortable like a bird that should migrate somewhere; a bird that lost its memory. Don't mind me, though. I will disappear soon and then all our troubles will be over. I shan't bother you. I might, though, sort of vanish inside you; wouldn't that be nice? [*He has been writing and hands* DAVID *the piece of paper.*] There you are, my son. Here is your revenge.

DAVID [*reads it and has difficulty*]: By the sound of it it should be very effective. Where did you learn about it?

SAM: Picked it up since I was buried. It's effective, don't you worry. Now go on, off with you; they're returning soon.

[DAVID *goes off into the house reading it.*]

He'll drink some, too; so will I. I hate unhappy endings. It'll work but not in the way that he expects.

[DAVID *is about to leave the house when* BLACK *stops him*.]

BLACK: Excuse me, sir, could I interest you in a very good life insurance policy?

DAVID: But I thought you sold tombstones?

BLACK: I used to, but you see I was never really . . . I'm a student of life.

DAVID: We must have a drink when I get back. I'm going to something very special; I'm sure after that you'll never be yourself again. [*Exits.*]

BLACK: Wonderful. What a charming boy! He's really turning out a decent sort.

[*There is a great commotion and the crowd of people come in the door.* BESSIE *and* SEGAL *come in arm in arm and dancing; they are already quite drunk.* MR *and* MRS STONE *follow. Then* HAVA, *who looks sad;* GREEN *and* WHITE *also enter.* MR STONE *starts the gramophone and plays a typical Hebrew melody and when* SAM *comes in it all seems to go a little quieter. There is much eating and drinking.*]

HAVA: It seems brighter here now.

BLACK [*to White and Green*]: Hello, you two back?

GREEN: Yes, we bumped into them. [*He is quite tipsy and takes hold of* BLACK *and guides him around the stage in a dreamy love attitude, to the music.*]

WHITE [*follows them around*]: I've got the money! [*He is cuddling a brown paper parcel.*]

[BESSIE *is talking seriously to* MRS STONE. *The* MEN *are now drinking around the table;* HAVA *is looking around the house.*]

BESSIE: I still can't help thinking that I got married too soon. I don't know – I feel it wasn't right.

[SAM *is also drinking.*]

MRS STONE: Don't worry yourself. It wasn't too soon. Enjoy yourself while there is still time. You're still a young girl. Years ago it might have been different but this is the age of the jet; everything is getting faster and faster.

HAVA: I don't think I've been in this house for a month.

[SEGAL, *who is very drunk, now stands on a chair.*]

SEGAL: Tonight, everyone, we are going to have a wonderful party. All Stepney Green is invited. A real old-fashioned party; dancing and singing. Forget wars, forget politics, and enjoy yourself.

HAVA [*goes to him*]: I'm so happy for you, Daddy. You've been such a worry to me.

SEGAL: I've got a beautiful wife and a beautiful daughter. [*He kisses both of them.*]

HAVA: I still don't like the idea of moving here.

MRS STONE: What a man he is; how romantic! Why can't you be like that?

STONE: I will be, when I get married again.

HAVA: I wonder where Davey is?

SEGAL: Maybe right now, dear old Sam is getting married to my Sarah; God rest her soul; isn't that a lovely thought?

[SAM *looks round uncomfortably as if he is being pursued.*]

SAM: God forgive you, Mr Segal, don't do me any favours. Bessie is an angel compared to your Sarah. If they gave me a choice of everlasting darkness or your Sarah, I would choose the darkness.

SEGAL [*sings*]: The second time is always nicer,
     And this is my second time.
     For many years I've been a miser,
     That has been my crime.
     Oy, Yoy, wish me joy,
     Tonight I am a lucky boy.
     The second time is so much nicer;
     This is my second time.

BESSIE: They'll say I didn't wait for long
    But a girl must take her chance.
    Solly is so nice and strong
    And Sam led me a dance;

Well, well, I'm in a spell,
Tonight I am a lucky girl.
The second time is so much nicer;
This is my second time.

THREE MEN: The second hand is whizzing round;
Soon we'll be on our way.
Our policies are really sound;
Sign one with us today.
Dance, sing, love, and laugh,
We'll make up your epitaph.
The second time is so much nicer;
I DIED OF LOVE TODAY.

MRS STONE: Well, well, Bessie girl, Solly's got you in his spell . . .

ALL [sing]: The second time is so much nicer;
This is their second time.

[They all return to little groups; DAVID returns and one can see him busy mixing the ingredients over by a side table; HAVA stands close to him but he does not see her.]

SAM: All right, Bessie, I wish you joy. Mr Segal, er – may I call you Solly now? Solly, Bessie, I wish you both joy. Drive each other mad; here's to your good health and please God by you. [He raises a glass to them and then he turns and looks in a mirror at himself.]

HAVA [to Bessie]: Please, er – Mrs – what can I call you?

BESSIE: Call me Aunty Bessie.

HAVA: Please Aunty, help me to know Davey. We can't go on like this.

BESSIE: Leave him alone; don't have much to do with him. He'll drive you mad.

SEGAL: That's all right. They're all a little mad where she came from; working out in the hot sun all day for no pay. Who in his right mind would do that?

[HAVA goes into the garden sadly; DAVID is pouring out the drinks. The MEN sit down to play cards and it becomes very quiet in the room;

everybody seems moody and only SAM *is happy.* BLACK *suddenly sees David; he leaves the game.*]

BLACK: Oh, there you are. Now what about that insurance policy? Our company believe that . . .

[DAVID *snubs him and* BLACK *moodily returns to the card game.*]

BESSIE: There you are. Come on, darling. Davey, come on. Kiss me and shake your Uncle Solly by the hand.

DAVID: Leave me alone. [*Turns his back.*]

[SAM *goes over to him and reasons with him.*]

SAM: Go on, Davey, play their game. It's nearly over. Wait and see what I've got in store for you.

DAVID: What?

BESSIE: There he goes, talking to himself again.

SAM: Just be patient. Kiss your mother, wish them joy. Give them all a drink [*he winks*] and Bob's your uncle.

[HAVA *has heard David talking and she comes into the doorway and stands there watching.*]

DAVID [*goes over to* BESSIE *and* SEGAL]: Mother, I wish you joy and happiness. [*Kisses her.*] Mr Segal, I hope that you'll be very happy. I would like you all to have a little drink with me; I would like to toast your health.

[DAVID *hands around the drinks to everyone. He is about to by-pass* SAM, *but* SAM *takes one.* DAVID *shrugs. He does not give* HAVA *a drink.*]

SEGAL: Thank you, thank you, thank God. Have you decided what you want to do yet?

DAVID: I'll talk to you about it tomorrow.

SEGAL: You mean you'll take over the herring stall? At last? [*To himself*] I can't stand those herrings any longer.

DAVID: No, I'm not. Tomorrow I'm going to leave home.

[*Everybody is despondent and* DAVID *raises his glass.*]

Here's to tomorrow. I wish you both joy. May this be the last of your worries, Lochiam. [*He raises the glass to his lips and is about to drink when he sees* HAVA; *lowers his glass and does not drink.*]

[*Everyone else drinks and as soon as they do they immediately start singing and dancing like mad. Everyone is in love with everyone else.* SAM *is trying to dance with* DAVID – MR *and* MRS STONE *are cuddling and kissing.*]

SAM [*thinking that* DAVID *has had a drink*]: Eh, Davey, what do you think of my love potion? Cabella, Smaballah, hahahhhah.

[*Everyone is dancing around in a ring and* WHITE *hands* DAVID *the parcel of money.*]

DAVID: What's this? Money? I don't want money, I want revenge. Here, take your money – confetti for the wedding.

[*He showers it over the stage and the others dance through it. The* THREE MEN *throw coloured streamers.* DAVID *looks at* HAVA, *who has been standing outside all this.*]

Oh? What's this? Oh, love, love, what a beautiful girl. I never realized how beautiful she is. Why haven't I seen her before? Who does she belong to?

SAM: She's yours.

[HAVA *goes into the garden.* DAVID *is very happy and now dances with* SAM.]

DAVID: Mine? What do you mean? Sam, oh my darling dear dead Sam. Life is a great time. [*sings*]:

> Life is the gayest time, life is the grandest time,
> Life is the greatest time to be together,
> So sing for all your worth, and learn to love your life,
> And dance upon the earth, and be my lover.
> Life is a dream of sight, life is a blessing bright,
> Life is the time of light, that's not for ever,
> It happens only once, so while we have a chance,
> Come on, let's sing and dance and be my lover.

[BESSIE *is collecting the money together. She hands it to* DAVID.]

DAVID: But I owe it to you – almost the whole of it.

BESSIE: I know, but take it with you – I don't need it.

DAVID: Thank you very much.

[*He looks at her for a while, then she returns to Segal. DAVID leads SAM to the garden where HAVA is sitting nearby.*]

DAVID [*to Sam*]: Is she really mine?

SAM: Exchange is no robbery.

DAVID: But who is she?

SAM: Solly Segal's daughter.

DAVID: I know, but apart from that? [*Calls into house.*] Hold everything! I've changed my mind about a lot of things. Do nothing until you hear from me.

SAM [*seeing the way DAVID is looking at Hava*]: Well, Davey, did my potion work or didn't it?

DAVID: I didn't drink any of that stuff [*goes right into the garden and approaches Hava.*]

SAM [*to the audience*]: So, exchange is no robbery. A Levy becomes a Segal and a Segal becomes a Levy.

[SAM *now hovers at the back of the garden. All noise and movement in the house stops. The garden scene becomes idyllic.*]

DAVID: There's so much that I want to tell you.

HAVA: There'll be a lot of time.

DAVID: All our lives. [*He kisses her.*] Isn't life wonderful? This is the happiest day of my life. What's your name?

HAVA: Hava.

DAVID: I daren't say it.

HAVA: Why not?

DAVID: If I say it I marry you.

HAVA: Well, say it then – you're the only boy for me. You always were and always will be.

DAVID: Hava! Hava! [*They kiss.*] I love you – why are you so different from any other girl?

HAVA: Why have you been so nasty . . . ? If you knew how long I waited just for a kind word.

DAVID: Sorry, Sweetheart, I've been too busy with myself – a very busy time I've had, but now I'm waking up.

HAVA: We used to play with each other when we were kids – then I went to Israel to get away from you but when I found you weren't there I came back again.

DAVID: I've been so mad – so crazy – how could I have missed someone so lovely as you – you're lovelier than my voice even.

HAVA: I wouldn't go so far as to say that.

DAVID: Why not – it's true – incredibly true.

HAVA: Oh, we'll get married and have lots of children – beautiful children with lovely voices – life will be wonderful . . .

DAVID: Life will be wonderful and life is wonderful – here we are on this little atlas – the world is a topical island in space – a bit of dust in time – and I own it and I give it to you – it doesn't matter where we are as long as we're happy.

HAVA: Oh, Davey – Davey – come down to earth a moment. How will we live? Your voice might enchant the gods, but we can't live on those kind of notes.

DAVID: But everything is all right – I've had a brainwave – I'll sell herrings and croon at the same time. Later I'll open a shop to be on the safe side – then I'll open another shop on the other side. What a gimmick! I'll be a sensation. I'll be the first singing herring salesman in history – I'll be terrific – I am terrific – A great success – the happiest crooner with the heart of gold.

[*Sings*]: A singer I must be, for all the world to see,

There's no one else like me, the whole world over.

I want to be a king – a great fantastic thing,

The boy with everything,

I love you, Hava.

[HAVA *smiles and hugs David for joy.*]

DAVID [*to Sam*]: Well, Dad, what did you think of that? Don't you think it's a marvellous idea? Me in the market: you can visit me there. Why didn't I think of it sooner?

[SAM *looks at the audience and shrugs.*]

SAM: Bravo, Davey boy, I'm pleased you're coming to your senses.

HAVA: Oh, dear, are you still talking to yourself?

DAVID: Oh, I'm not talking to myself; I'm talking to my father. I hope you don't mind?

HAVA: Will you be speaking to him for long? This father of yours?

DAVID: No, not for long.

HAVA: Oh, Davey, I'm so happy, all my dreams are coming true.

SAM: What a lucky boy you are, Davey. I envy you.

HAVA [to David]: I will not share you with anyone else.

DAVID: May I just have a few last words with him?

HAVA: Of course. I loved your father almost as much as my own.

SAM: Well, Davey, it's all over. Hamlet is dead and may flights of angels sing him down the stairs. He died two hours ago, when Mrs Levy became Mrs Segal; and I can go back whence I came.

DAVID: Are you revenged?

SAM: Certainly. You are the only Levy left in the world, but you are facing the right way. Segal is all right, moody and stingy; they will make an ideal couple. How subtle revenge can be! One last word of advice. I think you will be very happy, but try and remember me, commit arson every day in your imagination, burn down the previous day's lies, have a little revolution now and again in your heart; try and help lonely people. People are lonely all over the world; lonely and lovely because they are animals with souls and memories.

HAVA: Come on, Davey, let's get away from here.

DAVID: Are you saying good-bye to your father?

HAVA: No, not now.

[She cries softly, but everything else is silent.]

DAVID: Good-bye, father of mine. This, then, is your exorcism. Good-bye – I'll take the memory of you everywhere that I go.

[He tries to embrace Sam, but HAVA is tugging at him.]

SAM: That's what you think!

DAVID: Good-bye, Dad, go in peace. So long.

[DAVID leans upon the fence, head in his hands. HAVA comforts him. SAM dances towards the house, he is very gay.]

SAM: Good-bye, my boy; take care of your lovely girl. I'm going from Stepney Green and so are you. Your mother will move out from here and others will move in; they will cover the walls and floorboards and ceilings and then call it security. There will be nothing left of the places I knew. I will soar away from White-chapel, and follow all my dear dead friends. Look out for me now and again, even if I am not there. Whitechapel is curling up and going to sleep, and the Thames looks like a little trail of water running along the stones. All the names and faces I know are fading.

[*He is in the house and he dances among the people. As he does so they become animated again and dance round.* SAM *withdraws to the street door and he stands there.* BLACK *rushes to the garden.*]

Hava, David, Solly, Bessie. I'm so glad that there is going to be a happy ending. [*He stands in the open doorway.*]

[BLACK *touches David on the shoulder.*]

DAVID: Didn't you see him? Didn't you hear him?

HAVA: Yes, I almost saw him. I think I heard him.

BLACK [*gives card to him*]: David Levy, I think you have an excep-tional voice. With your gimmick, you'll go a long way. Come to my office Monday. I have a proposition for you.

DAVID: But you're not an agent?

BLACK: No, but I'm going to be. I'll start with you. We'll work out something. I'm a student of life. If we put our heads together, plus a little money, the world will hear you.

[BLACK *returns into the house.*]

HAVA: Wonderful, marvellous; come, let's go. Where shall we go to?

DAVID: Let's go to a dance.

HAVA: Life is going to be one long dance; you've got two hundred pounds, let's go and find a place to live.

DAVID: Why do you love me?

HAVA: Because I have no choice. Why do you love me?

DAVID: Because I love you.

[*They kiss, laugh heartily and exit ecstatically, laughing and kissing.*]

SAM: They are not really themselves. I'm going now, my children, to regions unknown – enjoy yourselves. Make the most of your youth – because youth is a wreath of roses – make the most of your life – because life is a holiday from the dark – make the most of the world – because it is *YOUR WORLD* – because the world is a wedding – so – Let the wedding continue –

[*He shrugs and smiles and as the room animates again and the people dance, he holds out his arms to the audience and then turns and quickly goes.*]

[*The* CHILDREN *are heard singing.*]

CHILDREN [*off*]: Now you're married I wish you joy,

        First a girl, then a boy,

        Kiss her once, kiss her twice,

        Kiss her three times over . . .

[*There is a great gust of laughter as the curtain falls.*]

THE END OF THE PLAY

[*After curtain falls the cast line up and sing.*]

DAVID: I am the boy who wanted to be king – see me on the tele – please God by me – please God by you.

HAVA: I am the girl who owns the boy – who wanted to be king – does anyone know of a flat in Golders Green – please God by me – please God by you.

SAM: I am the ghost who was haunted by my life, wasn't lucky enough to love someone like this girl – who owns my only son – who wanted to be king – I'll be seeing you all – please God by me – please God by you.

BESSIE: I am the wife who drove her husband mad so he became the ghost who wants to pinch the girl who owns my little boy who wanted to be king – God bless him – it's enough to give you heartburn – still – please God by me – please God by you.

SEGAL: I am the friend who jumped into the bed to comfort poor Bessie who drove Sam to his grave – so he became a ghost with designs on my daughter – why the dirty dog – I'm glad she's out of danger – and now she owns the boy who wanted to be king – my mad stepson – still I wish them joy – Comrades, down with religion – please God by me – please God by you.

MR STONE: I am the cabbie – believe me, business ain't so good – I drove the Prime Minister the other day – he didn't give me a tip – please God by me – please God by you.

MRS STONE: I am his wife – enough has been said – by my life – by your life – the children of today – please God by your daughter – please God by your son – please God by God – please God by me – please God by you.

THREE: We are the salesmen, the backbone of the nation – may we press our stones upon you in our never-never fashion – Hip, Hip, Hooray, we haven't got a clue – please God – for he's a jolly good fellow – please God by you.